CENTRAL ASIAN RESPONSES
TO RADICAL ISLAM

Evgueni K. Novikov

American Foreign Policy Council
Washington DC
December 2006

TABLE OF CONTENTS

ACKNOWLEDGMENTS

A number of people inspired and assisted my work on this project. They include: Dr. Samantha Ravich, who saw the value of this effort from the start, and urged me to proceed with its implementation; Dr. Nadia Schadlow, whose kind advice helped me to put the project's ideas into practice; Clinton I. Smullyan, board member of the Jamestown Foundation, whose financial support helped make it possible; Dr. Orozbek Moldaliev, professor of the Kyrgyzstan Diplomatic Academy, who helped me to understand the nature of Central Asia's potential contribution to the fight against Wahhabi ideology; Todd Leventhal, who provided me with indispensable editorial and intellectual advice and support; Ilan Berman, Vice President of the American Foreign Policy Council, whose energy and experience helped organize work on the project; and American Foreign Policy Council President Herman Pirchner, for his support and supervision.

ABOUT THE AUTHOR

EVGUENI K. NOVIKOV is Visiting Fellow in Islamic Studies at the American Foreign Policy Council in Washington, DC. He is also a Senior Fellow of the Jamestown Foundation.

An expert on Islam and on the politics and economics of the Persian Gulf region, Dr. Novikov was born in Kyrgyzstan of Russian parents. He received his Master's degree in Business and Foreign Trade in the Gulf States from the Moscow State Institute of International Relations, and his Ph.D. in the politics and economy of Arabic countries from the Moscow Institute of Social Sciences.

Dr. Novikov has extensive practical experience in Central Asia and the Persian Gulf region. As an elite Soviet expert on Islamic affairs, his responsibilities over the years ranged from instruction in the theory and practice of socialism to students from Islamic countries to advising Arab leaders on political affairs, international relations and trade issues. His official duties as a representative of the Soviet Communist Party's International Department provided Dr. Novikov with the opportunity to establish close personal and working relationships with many high-ranking officials in Islamic republics, including Yemen, Iraq and Kuwait.

Following his defection to the United States in 1988, Dr. Novikov served on the faculty of the U.S. Naval War College and of the George C. Marshall European Center for Security Studies in Germany, where he instructed pro-democracy leaders of the then newly independent nations of Central Asia.

INTRODUCTION

More than five years after September 11, it is fair to say that the U.S. government remains challenged by how to combat the ideology of radical Islamists. In some ways, this is not surprising. The West now faces a challenge in an area—religious controversy—which the modern state prefers to leave to individual discretion, and in which it is not accustomed to contend. Moreover, the struggle is taking place within a largely unfamiliar religion, in an area in which the West is, at best, tone-deaf. Nevertheless, this new "battle of ideas" must be joined and won if the United States is to address what have become grave threats to its security.

The ideas of radical Islamists are growing in popularity today among Muslims not because they are correct or have such irresistible inherent appeal, but because the government of Saudi Arabia has expended enormous resources over the span of more than three decades in order to support them, and because advocates of moderate Islam have not been able to match these contributions. As America searches for a way to effectively wage the "battle of ideas" against this ideology, known as Wahhabism, tapping into the expertise of those in Central Asia who are successfully waging this battle, and applying their lessons more widely, can help to fill some of the gaping holes in current U.S. strategy.

Before September 11, the United States paid little attention to Wahhabi ideology, which has spread all over the Muslim world and became a major component in shaping the agenda of Islamic terrorist organizations. According to Freedom House, the "Wahhabi sect, which would have been regarded as recently as fifty years ago as an austere, fringe group by a large majority of Muslims, is now extremely powerful and influential in the Muslim world due to Saudi government support and the oil wealth of the Arabian peninsula."[1] Since the 1970s, the Saudi government has provided about $90 billion to the Wahhabis for spreading their ideology of hatred around the world.[2] This money has supported thousands of religious schools and colleges in Muslim countries that spread the Wahhabi vision of Islam and advocate Islamic "holy war" against infidels, mostly Americans and U.S. allies. In addition, Saudi money finances hundreds of print and electronic publications that promote this ideology of hatred, thereby helping to brainwash new recruits for terrorist organizations.

In the aftermath of the September 11 attacks, the United States has realized that it can not avoid the battle of ideas against Wahhabism. But, as the final report of the task force on public diplomacy chaired by Edward Djerejian noted, "America has not excelled in the struggle of ideas in the Arab and Muslim world. What is required is not merely tactical adaptation but strategic, and radical, transformation."[3]

U.S. strategy against militant Islamists should be based on a clear understanding of how Wahhabis misuse Islamic theology and implant an incorrect vision of Islam in the minds of people in the Arab and Muslim worlds. The United States needs to discredit the core ideas of Wahhabism, and demonstrate that its proponents deny the word and the spirit of true Islam and abuse the accepted wisdom of the Koran and the teaching of the Prophet Muhammad.

One major problem facing U.S. participants in the "battle of ideas" is finding the most effective ways to communicate and influence Muslim audiences. It is important to remember that Muslims and Arabs are more likely to acknowledge criticisms of Wahhabism as legitimate if these criticisms are made by Muslim scholars and experts. Indeed, many Muslims and Arabs tend to discount criticisms of militant Islamist ideology by Western experts on Islam as attacks on Islam's sacred spiritual heritage by "infidels."

In order to more effectively communicate with Arabs and Muslims, the United States should examine the arguments of Muslim scholars who advocate tolerant Islam. Since Wahhabi ideology is at odds with mainstream Islam, such scholars have their own reasons to speak out against proponents of militant Islam. The U.S. policy community should study the arguments such scholars and clerics have developed in places such as the republics of Central Asia. These moderate Muslims have developed ways to counter Wahhabi ideology that rely on the traditions and concepts of local, tolerant Islam. Most Central Asian Muslims are champions of the Hanafi strain of Islam, which is much older and has far greater authority within the Islamic world than does Wahhabism. Their quarrel with Wahhabism is based on a very precise knowledge of the Koran and the Hadith, the sayings of the Prophet—a kind of knowledge that is very rare among Western experts.

American politicians and journalists should, at a minimum, be aware of the critique of Wahhabism that is offered by Central Asian Muslims. A better understanding of the language, arguments, discussion methods, theological sources, images, allegories, and examples being used in the Central Asian struggle against radical Islam can inform U.S. public diplomacy and American efforts to support more moderate strains of Islam throughout the world. Central Asian scholars, policymakers and activists are working to find ways to defeat the advocates of Wahhabism on their own turf—the knowledge of original Islamic ideas—and thereby demolish their distorted vision of Islam. Likewise, by examining how Central Asia fights Wahhabism and its Saudi supporters, Americans can better understand how to shape effective aid programs in key Muslim regions in order to make moderate Muslims more successful, and to give Muslim opponents of militant Islamism a more powerful voice than that which they currently have.

WHY THE CENTRAL ASIAN EXPERIENCE IS IMPORTANT

Long before September 11th, Central Asian governments had recognized the danger that radical Islamists posed to their existence. More than a decade ago, the scholars Roald Sagdeev and Susan Eisenhower had already noted that "Uzbekistan with its authoritarian secular regime... is the main obstacle to the expansion of Islamic fundamentalism in the region."[4] Indeed, Uzbekistan and other Central Asian governments have undertaken tough administrative measures against adherents of radical Islam, often violating international human rights standards in the process.[5] This has posed a dilemma for the United States and its efforts to promote democracy in region. Washington certainly does not wish to condone or approve of such methods, but neither should it wish to undermine regional governments in their struggle against radical Islam, which is even less likely to honor human rights. Very often, the result has been a form of policy paralysis and avoidance.

None of this, however, diminishes the important steps Central Asian governments have taken to de-legitimize the Wahhabi ideology, to limit its ideological influence on local Muslims, and to "immunize" the hearts and minds of local youth against the appeal of radical Islamist organizations and terrorist groups. Central Asian governments, especially those in Uzbekistan and Kyrgyzstan, have developed an educational system—from kindergarten through the university level—that inculcates the moral norms and social principles of tolerant Islam, and that respects the value of any human life (Muslim, Christian, Jewish, or other). That system provides textbooks for schools, cartoons for children, education for imams of local mosques, a network of counselors in Islamic affairs for central and local administrations, and television and radio talk shows that challenge the Wahhabi interpretation of the Koran and Hadith and provide listeners with an alternative, moderate, religious vision. Similarly, these governments have created a network of educational establishments and research centers that champion the tolerant and peaceful ideas of Islam and condemn Wahhabi ideas. Students of *madrassas* and universities in Tashkent and Bishkek study Arabic intensively, and upon graduation not only can read and interpret the Koran and Hadith, but also teach in Arabic. Graduates of these educational establishments become knowledgeable imams for mosques and theology teachers for public schools. Yet most American analysts, primarily influenced by concerns about the shortcomings of the Central Asian governments in the human rights arena, are not aware of these important initiatives.

Today, the United States and Central Asian governments share a common enemy—radical Islam—and U.S. policy makers can learn valuable lessons for the battle of ideas from Central Asian religious leaders, academic researchers and governmental officials, who have much practical experience in fighting Wahhabism and winning the hearts and minds of Islamic audiences. These governments have been successful in dealing with extremism, and Americans should bring their experience to bear in the larger "battle of ideas" with radical Islam taking place throughout the Muslim world. The advantages Central Asia can offer are manifold:

- In these majority-Muslim countries, the Hanafi branch of Sunni Islam is the one with the strongest influence on the local population. The teachings of Abu Hanafi are the most tolerant and the most liberal among the main schools of Islam. Its tolerance and deliberate distancing from politics are one of the main reasons that Hanafi believers survived and avoided mass repressions during the Communist era.

- During 70 years of Communist rule in Central Asia, local Muslims were isolated from the external Muslim world: while permitting local Muslims to keep their faith, Soviet ideologists did not want any competition for

Marxism-Leninism from Islam or any other theology. Hanafi religious leaders had a chance to continue teaching inside a few officially permitted mosques and educational centers, while the general public maintained its Islamic faith and culture in the household, having no access to formal Islamic education. During the Soviet era, "being Muslim" was a tool of self-identification for people of Central Asia, a niche to escape from totalitarian communist ideological control.

- After gaining independence, these countries managed to educate considerable numbers of very knowledgeable experts in Islam. The Koran and Hadith have been translated into local languages, and many local academics and imams are applying their knowledge on a practical level.

- The level of anti-Americanism among the Central Asian states is low compared to other Muslim countries, and for good reason. In spite of the current official anti-American propaganda, the older generation has fond memories of America's struggle with the Soviet Union, while the younger generation has seen few negative examples of U.S. behavior in their countries, and many examples of American achievement (i.e.., computers, business, car manufacture, music and films).

- Moreover, these countries were isolated from the rest of the Muslim world for most of the 20th Century, and local people do not identify themselves with a greater Muslim ummah. They supported American actions in Afghanistan and are not greatly concerned about American operations in Iraq.

By contrast, the ideological foundations of Wahhabism are meager, and can be reduced to a few cornerstones such as "denouncing Western democracy," "declaring that Muslim clergy should rule the state," "hatred of the United States," "call for holy war—*jihad*," "glorification of suicide and suffering for the cause of Islam," "blame and damnation of modern education and science," "depriving women of civil rights," and "a ban on modern films and television programs." All of these positions are justified by citing specific passages of the Koran, Hadith and other core sources of the Muslim faith. Because in Islam the right to interpret these sources does not belong to any "Muslim Vatican," and because any knowledgeable and respectful Muslim has the right to interpret the viii

Koran and Hadith, the opinions of Central Asian experts in Islam can be useful in challenging Wahhabi ideas.

In this book Central Asian religious leaders, academic researchers and governmental officials share their experience of the battle of ideas against Wahhabi ideology. They summarize their vision, methods, and practical approaches to fighting Wahhabism and Saudi influence. They are lessons worth learning.

THE ISLAMIC HERITAGE OF
THE CENTRAL ASIAN STATES

Since antiquity, the two sociological features most important to Central Asian people have been the clan (a tribe of nomads or an agricultural village led by one of its members) and the state (a central apparatus headed by a monarch-emir). As in any ancient Eastern society, the relationship between the clans and the state was predicated upon the strength of the state and the subservience of the clan members and was primarily political rather than economic in nature. The social compact provided that the central authority did not interfere in the social or economic life of the people. Nomads went about raising their cattle and agricultural clans their crops without regulation from state institutions or the monarch, although the people were required to pay taxes, which were sometimes substantial. These taxes, collected through military and political pressure on the clans, went directly to the monarch and his officials. In return, the state's military forces were obliged to protect the taxpayers from foreign enemies and to intercede in tribal feuds.

Because economic relations between the state and the clans—as well as those between the clans themselves—were underdeveloped, the elements of Central Asian society were not interdependent, and the inner life of each proceeded virtually uninfluenced by the others. The state apparatus was erected in cities and towns, where officials permitted the existence of craftsmen and merchants. Peasants spent most of their lives in the villages; some never left them at all. In extreme situations, such as foreign aggression against the state, the monarch could call clan members—both peasants and nomads—to join his fighting forces, but as soon as the war was over, they went back to their homes.

At the time Islam began to penetrate Central Asia, there were more than 15 states that periodically fought against each other on that territory, then called Maverannahra (Arabic for "the other side of the river," that is, north of the Amu Darya River, which divides present-day Afghanistan from the former Soviet Union). Sharp differences also existed between some of the tribes, such as the settled agricultural clans and Turkic nomads. Feuds were often based on religious differences; there were numerous tribal religions, loyalties to which

2

prevented the peaceful coexistence of the different tribes, clans, and states of Maverannahra.

Numerous "temples of fire" and "temples of idols" existed in Central Asia, according to ancient sources, and each home in Bukhara sheltered an idol whose image was engraved on the entrance.[6] The nomads of pre-Islamic Central Asia believed in Heaven as the ultimate idol.[7] Zoroastrianism was also widely practiced in Maverannahra; Buddhism had its followers, too. In fact, the name Bukhara is thought to have originated from the word *vahara*—"Buddhist temple."[8]

In contrast to the fragmentation that existed, Islam offered the means to unify disparate tribal clans into a unified community loyal to a belief common to all. Islamic doctrines were first enunciated by the founder of Islam, Muhammad, in the middle of the seventh Century and were instrumental in uniting the Arabian tribes, which had been as fragmented as those in Central Asia.

Introduced by invading Arabs into Central Asia late in the seventh Century A.D., by "the tenth Century Islam [had become] the religion of Central Asia, with just a small group of Bukharan Jews resisting the onslaught. From this time on, Central Asia became one of the most prestigious cultural centers of the Dar ul-Islam (the World of Islam)."[9]

CENTRAL ASIA'S UNDERSTANDING OF ISLAMIC PRINCIPLES

Westerners generally do not understand how far Islam exceeds their expectations of what a religion should encompass. While it is, of course, concerned with a believer's personal relations with God and his ethical behavior within the community, Islam also imposes a culture, dictates a system of laws, and establishes the basis for the functioning of a state. Taking all of its pronouncements together, Islam guides all aspects of daily life from birth to death. It is necessary to comprehend this totality of involvement in people's thoughts and activities in order to clearly view the Muslim situation today.

Any resident of Central Asia being instructed in the ways of Islam today is taught the same principles that Central Asians learned in the seventh Century. The foundation of Islamic faith rests on the acceptance that Allah is the one God, that Muhammad was His prophet, the carrier of His message and will, and that nothing happens in this world unless Allah wills it. The Qur'an is Islam's holy book, composed of sacred writings accepted by Muslims as revelations made to Muhammad by Allah through the angel Gabriel.

All the requirements of the religion are listed in the following verse of the Qur'an:

> O ye who believe! Believe in God and His Prophet, and the scripture which He sent to those before [Him]. Any who denieth God, His angels, His Books, His Prophets, and the Day of Judgment, hath gone far, far astray. (4:136)

The procedure for accepting Islam is uncomplicated: in the presence of witnesses, one commits oneself entirely and without reservation to the religion ("Islam" in Arabic means "giving oneself," "submission," or "surrender") by pronouncing the short creed, "There is no God but Allah and Muhammad is His Prophet!", after which one becomes a member of the Muslim faith and can receive the privileges reserved for Islam's followers. Allah is merciful and just and promises Paradise to all those who are committed to the faith. A Muslim will find there all the material things that he has perhaps not enjoyed on Earth: good food, fine wines, many wives, and a nice house.

According to Islamic dogma, human nature is not inherently sinful. And humans are not responsible for the first sin of Adam: the Qur'an teaches that Allah forgave Adam for his transgression and guided him in the correct way. Islam does not favor asceticism and does not encourage people to give up earthly pleasures for the better life in Heaven; it strongly opposes a monkish or an unmarried life. A faithful Muslim should indulge every pleasure in his life on earth—as long as he does not go beyond the boundaries of the law and he remembers Allah by consistently fulfilling several commandments.

There are five pillars of Islam, the duties that Muslims are required to consistently carry out to show their individual willingness to fulfill the will of God and their loyalty to their strong community united in the fellowship of faith: reaffirm faith once each day by reciting the short creed (*shahadah*), pray five times daily facing Mecca (*salat*), show concern for the poor by giving alms (*zakat*), fast during the month of Ramadan (*sawm*), and at least once in a lifetime make the pilgrimage to the holy shrine Kaaba in Mecca (the Hajj). Sometimes considered an additional duty is *jihad*, the concept of which has been variously interpreted over the years. Taken literally, "striving in the way of God," its meanings have ranged from simply trying to fulfill the ethical norms and principles of the Qur'an to entering into holy war in defense of Islam.

But the commandments are flexible. Although the daily ritual prayers are preferably recited in a mosque, if a Muslim cannot go to one, he can pray anywhere he likes. Further, he does not have to use the services of a professional priest (mullah) if he has no access to such mullah; a Muslim believes he communicates directly with Allah, telling him about personal problems and asking Him for help in solving them. Any respected Muslim who knows the basic elements of the religion can lead a service.

The Muslim month of fasting is observed during one lunar month a year, when the faithful should not eat, drink, or smoke from dawn to sunset; before sunrise and at night, they are free of restrictions. Travelers, old people, anyone who is ill, pregnant women, women who are breast-feeding, and all those who are engaged in heavy work are excused from the fast.

A newly-admitted Muslim is exempt from paying individual taxes to the state (*jizya*). The requirement to give alms is satisfied if an adult Muslim donates 2.5 percent of his income from real estate, trade, and business; he is expected to give to the poor, to dervishes, and to mosques. This charity is an essential part of the ritual for saving one's soul and the forgiveness of sins.

The Hajj is obligatory for the wealthy but not for the poor. As a matter of fact, over time and due to the Soviet authorities' restrictions for Soviet citizens to travel abroad, Central Asia has acquired its own sacred place-tombs of famous Central Asian Muslims. During Soviet times, pilgrimages to these tombs counted as the Hajj for Muslims in Central Asia.

The framework of Islamic law comes from the Shari'ah—in Arabic, "the correct path to the goal." The Shari'ah has four sources: the Qur'an; the Sunnah, "the standard or model to follow" as reported in a collection of hadiths, or traditional stories about the Prophet Muhammad's actions, deeds, and statements in different life situations; the consensus of the community of believers (*ijma*); and analogy (*qiyas*), or applying the reasoning by which past decisions were made to new situations. Islam demands that Muslims not only be faithful to the dogmas of the Qur'an but also strictly comply with Shari'ah norms, rules of behavior, structures that organize society, and regulations and canons, which have the force of laws. The legal system is complicated: it deals with all kinds of family, property, commercial, moral, legal, and personal relationships; and it affirms the brotherhood of Muslims, their equality, their freedom, and the principles of Muslim justice.

Interpretations of Shari'ah norms and regulations have differed from one country to another, from one period to another, even as to whether they are subject to interpretation at all or should be obeyed as immutable commandments.

THE ACCEPTANCE AND SPREAD OF ISLAM IN CENTRAL ASIA

As a result of the Arab invasion, Central Asia gradually became a centralized Muslim state. This put an end to the frequent wars in the region, which contributed to stability and prosperity for all, especially poor people, as well as security for their property. The Arabs did not interfere with their lives and levied taxes that were lower than those paid to the smaller states before.

Islam spread rapidly in Central Asia because it was readily acceptable to all levels of the population. For instance, the Arabs permitted local rulers to choose the administrators of the state, who in turn approved of Islam because not only had they not lost power but the new religion actively blessed their secular authority. It is easy to see why local monarchs, chiefs of different tribes, and heads of various clans gladly supported Islam.

Poor peasants were the majority of the population. They depended on state administrators and landlords, who possessed land and controlled the all-important water. They were drawn to Islam because it promised equality of the poor and the rich in the eyes of Allah and added a certain dignity to their lives. Nomads and peasants also found reassurance in Islam, according to one scholar, because it did not require them to break from their kin; the new religion simply gave equal respect to social and political relationships, leaving clan solidarity untouched.[10]

The urban population, in large part merchants, also embraced Islam. Central Asian merchants traded with local tribes and were also involved in the international trade between the Far East and Europe, which was channeled through the largest intermediary centers of that time, Bukhara and Sogd (modern Samarkand). They favored the existence of a strong central government because it would free them from the dictates of numerous sovereigns; they viewed the new religion as a viable means to create and maintain such a government and state. Moreover, Islam has a positive attitude towards merchants and trade; it protects private property unequivocally and praises active and entrepreneurial people. The Qur'an says:

> Not equal are those believers who sit [at home] and receive no hurt, and those who strive and fight in the cause of God with their goods and their persons. God hath granted a grade higher to those who strive and fight with their goods and persons than to those who sit [at home]. Unto all [in faith] hath God promised good: but those who strive and fight hath He distinguished above those who sit [at home]. (4:26)

Having received this sort of support from the new religion, a merchant or a property owner who had accumulated capital through his own activities did not have to worry about threats to his position in society. Previously, people envied—even condemned—a merchant who had acquired wealth and in hard times gave him no help or sympathy. Under Islam, he became a respected member of society, and his trade was considered beneficial and blessed by Allah.

Thus Islam was a "convenient" religion for different segments of Central Asian society for socioeconomic and political reasons. It adapted itself to the life of the local population, absorbing their beliefs and customs while uniting them. As it is described in the Qur'an, "God doth wish to make clear to you and to show you the ordinances of those before you." (4:26)

By the fourteenth century, the centralized Central Asian state had become quite prosperous, with Islam still very much a part of its political system and culture, and it became a target for Mongol invasion. While the Mongols succeeded in conquering Central Asia militarily and ruling it politically, the invaders were themselves conquered culturally as they became assimilated into local society and converted to Islam.

Even at the beginning of its world expansion, Islam proved capable of taking into consideration a variety of local cultures, giving a new interpretation to old ideas, rapidly adjusting to local conditions, considering the realities of everyday life, and being racially absorbent, tolerant, and patient. Therefore, Islam in Central Asia, both in the early days of expansion and subsequently, always included various pre-Islamic traditions. New generations of Central Asian Muslims, the modern population included, viewed these old customs as blessed by Islam and as an indigenous part of Islamic doctrine. This ability of Islam to adapt to local conditions and its usefulness in solving social problems account for its quick and easy assimilation into Central Asia and for Islam's continuing influence there today.

Having become an essential part of traditional Central Asian society, Islam actively contributed to its consolidation. The language of the Qur'an, which created a foundation for literary Arabic, influenced the evolution of the Turkic languages of the Central Asian people. Almost half of the words in these languages have Arabic roots; until Soviet times, all of their alphabets were Arabic.

As a religion for all tribes and clans living in that territory, Islam created a uniform system of values, norms of public behavior, rituals for ceremonies, and legal rules for relationships. Members of tribal communities never forgot their ties to home and family, but through Islam they could widen their perspective and forge a common bond with other tribes and kinship-based groups. A new spirit of national consciousness was born from the notion of affiliation between one's own tribe or kin and the larger world of Islam—one's tribe was close to or related to another tribal community if both shared Islamic beliefs.

This budding national consciousness was further aided by the fact that the majority of Central Asian Muslims belonged to the same denomination, Sunni Islam, and to the Hanafi school of thought. (The original body of Islam had split relatively early, when leadership was disputed among the followers of various descendants of Muhammad. Of the two major branches, Sunni and Shiite Muslims, the larger is the Sunni; the Shiites have fragmented further over the years, while the Sunni have been more stable and continued to honor the original philosophy. While the several branches of Islam believe that they belong to one Muslim nation, the *ummah*, the differences among them are substantial enough that they can hardly be called united.)

Thus, by breaking down the ethnic boundaries between the different tribal communities of Central Asia, Islam became not just a religion but also a factor that determined most aspects of their individual, social, political, and economic lives.

RUSSIAN DOMINATION

When the expanding Russian Empire reached Central Asia with significant forces in the mid-1800s (there had been incursions since the sixteenth Century), it met only "sporadic resistance. The native principalities, Bukhara, Khiva, and Kokand... were unable to oppose the overwhelming might of the Czarist Empire." [11] One by one, areas fell under Russian domination. "The conquest of Central Asia was rounded off with the occupation of the Turkmen territory between 1873 and 1884... and the annexation of the eastern part of the Pamir in 1900." [12] Central Asia became known as Russian Turkestan and, except for the Khanate of Khiva and the Emirate of Bukhara which had accepted protectorate status, was administered by a Russian authority, the governor general of Turkestan. This ended the isolation of the Islamic societies there and brought them into direct contact with European civilization.

Russia intentionally constrained the high-ranking Islamic clergy whose positions were part of the government structure (which we call, as a body, "official Islam"). They were not allowed to maintain ties with the outside Muslim world, which kept them from being influenced by reformist influences that were developing in Muslim countries, such as Turkey, that had opened themselves to Western civilization.

Central Asian Muslims were still part of the larger sphere of Islam in that, as Alexandre Bennigsen and Marie Broxup explained in their book on Russian/ Soviet interactions with Islam, "for centuries, the Muslim territories of Central Asia... maintained the closest possible contact with the rest of the Muslim world, sharing as they did the same culture and history, being ruled by the same dynasties, and speaking and writing the same language." Even the increasing influence of Russia in Central Asia "did not fundamentally change this situation, for even as late as the nineteenth Century ideas, political doctrines, and individuals were constantly moving back and forth over the Czarist Empire's southern borders with the Ottoman Empire, Iran, and Muslim India. [In the early 1900s]... Samarqand still belonged to the Dar Ul-Islam and was closer to Tabriz and Isfahan than to Moscow or Petrograd."[13]

CENTRAL ASIAN SOCIETY BEFORE THE COMMUNIST REVOLUTION

The structure of Central Asian society at the start of the twentieth century can best be understood by examining the example of the Emirate of Bukhara, where the Islamic model of organizing the life of the state had been realized most completely. As in the rest of Central Asia, the emirate was a society in which Islam held the dominant position, and clerical and secular powers were fully integrated.

An emir, a descendant of the Prophet Muhammad, headed the government. Bukhara was part of a Muslim state ruled by a caliph—at that time, the caliph for the Muslims of Central Asia was the Sultan of Turkey—and it was as the caliph's surrogate that the emir ruled over about 2.5 million people, half of them Uzbeks, one-third Tajiks, and one-tenth Turkmen.

The emirate was a large territory, part of the immense plain between the Syr Darya and Amu Darya rivers to the north and southwest and the Kyzyl Kum desert and Pamir Mountains to the northwest and east. The cities of Bukhara and Samarkand, which had been ancient trade centers on the Silk Road from the orient to the west, were located in the rich valley of the Zeravshan River.

Michael Rywkin, an American historian, described one facet of life in the emirate:

> The political structure was medieval. The land... was most often cultivated by impoverished tenants who were allowed to retain only between one-half and one-fifth of the crop. Irrigation, essential in the area, was under the control of state functionaries. Many peasants were landless... Slavery existed throughout the territory.[14]

Only the rules of Shari'ah limited the emir's power; he was the highest authority for all the people in his realm. As Russian historian A.A. Seminov put it, "He granted privileges and favors, which were much sought after, but he was also a greatly feared ruler whose anger destroyed many people and ruined their fortunes."[15]

The second in command in the emirate was the *Shaykh-ul-Islam* (head of Islam), who was the highest ranking of the Muslim clergy. Third in line was the *kazi-kalan*, the chief justice; he was the judge of the city of Bukhara and was responsible for all the justices of the kingdom.

The emir not only headed the Bukharan government, he also ruled on all issues related to Islam and appointed or dismissed the members of the clergy (both the leaders and the ordinary), the judges, and the teachers at the *madrassas* (religious schools), the Muslim seminaries. His power rested in the numerous Muslim clergymen who exercised control over the entire society of the Bukharan emirate. They were ubiquitous; in the city of Bukhara itself, there was one Muslim priest for every 30 people, or one for every ten adults 20 years or older.[16]

The clergy was unified, almost clannish, and even the emir had to take their formidable power into consideration; he would alter a ruling if he had made it without consulting the clergy and they subsequently expressed opposition. The Muslim clergy also possessed significant economic power, thanks to their ownership of endowments, private property and real estate. In the cities, they owned various handicraft shops, grocery stores, open markets, and taverns; in the villages, cultivated land, irrigation facilities, mills, and the like. One part of the profits from the endowments went to the maintenance of religious and charitable institutions; another was distributed among mosques, Muslim scholars, and teachers at the *madrassas*.

The numerous students at the *madrassas* were an important part of the clergy's social base. The students' views were sought in the selection of candidates for election to the highest offices in the kingdom, including the *kazi-kalan*. Their opinions influenced the clergy's decisions to dismiss certain officials in the kingdom or to countermand one of the emir's decrees. Teachers at the *madrassas* therefore tried to befriend the scholars, and high state officials sought their support.[17]

The Muslim clergy had power and influence beyond the high echelons of authority in the kingdom. No less significant were the rank-and-file ecclesiastics, the imams of *mahalla* (city quarter) mosques and village mosques in rural areas, who played an important, although not always highly visible, role among the

people. They ran the everyday activities of the local mosques and were also expected to gain new converts to Islam.

The imam of a city mosque was one of the most respected and powerful people in his neighborhood. He was a scholar of the Shari'ah and its interpreter for any of his congregation who were illiterate. The imam had significant influence on local opinion; he could accuse or clear a man based upon the strictures of the Shari'ah and announce his decision. He was the spiritual leader of his congregation and a judge of their morals. The imam was required to participate in the most significant events in the lives of the people; he registered marriages and births, prayed for the sick, conducted funerals, and so on. In most cases, he also taught at the local school and thus had influence on the younger generation as well.

A village imam was usually the only literate person among the people and thus served as the only link between the village and the outside world. The common folk trusted him as the only one who could read and interpret the Qur'an, which was the source of wisdom and undisputed truth for any Muslim when he decided to initiate an important venture. A Muslim who was about to marry or divorce, buy or sell a house, start a long journey, or begin sowing or harvesting went first to find out from the Qur'an if he would be successful in his undertaking. If the Qur'an said he would not, he usually decided not to proceed.[18]

The village imam's activities went far beyond presiding over and regulating the religious activities of his congregation. He actively participated in governing the community and had a decisive vote in all matters; he even took part in collecting taxes. He was the chief counsel for the villagers on all vital issues, the teacher of their children, and often the chief physician of the village. People asked his advice on all the most important issues, "starting from purchasing a donkey, all the way through marriages of their sons and daughters, and repairing their old samovars."[19]

But his standing among the villagers was solid also because his position was not forced on the citizens by anyone. The imam did not receive an official salary but lived off voluntary contributions from his congregation as well as the fees he earned for certain religious duties that he performed, such as weddings and funerals. There was also a special tax in the emirate of Bukhara to benefit the local imams, the so-called *mushtak* (handful), from which he was paid with food.

The Muslim community, the *ummah*, in Bukhara as well as in other regions of Central Asia, was a strong, interrelated structure that included a number of estates that were subordinated according to strict Islamic hierarchy. Even more closely knit than Christian communities, the members of the Central Asian *ummah* were united by their dervish organizations and Sufi orders. The elders— *ishans*—were their informal leaders. According to A. A. Seminov, these leaders exercised significant influence over the members of the community. Moreover, the elders dealt with every member of the community, regardless of their wealth or position in secular society. Important industrialists sat alongside common craftsmen and shabby unskilled workers during meetings in the *ishans'* homes. The accessibility of the *ishans*, their courtesy, and their readiness to help people in need won the admiration of all members of the community.[20]

PEOPLE OF OTHER RELIGIONS IN BUKHARA

Not all of the people in Central Asia were Muslims; there were Russian Christians, Jews, and Hindus who lived in the region and had to get along in an unfriendly Muslim environment. According to Shari'ah law, all people of a different religion who lived in the emirate of Bukhara were considered *dhimmis* (outsiders, strangers). They had the right to perform their own religious activities, conduct business among themselves, and engage in relationships that were regulated by the civil law of their respective religions, but in criminal law issues and in business activities with Muslims, they were obligated to follow the laws of the Shari'ah. The *dhimmis* did not have the right to marry Muslims or to have Muslim slaves. They were belittled or stigmatized in any number of ways: restrictions on clothing, public behavior, where and what kind of homes they could build; they were even forbidden to ride horses (they were allowed donkeys or mules).[21]

Other commandments in the Qur'an complicated relationships between persons of different religions in the states of Central Asia: members of certain religions were not welcome to convert to Islam, and there were various restrictions on bequeathing and inheriting property.[22] If a spouse became a Muslim, a judge would force the other to convert by threatening to invalidate the marriage. Muslims were permitted to buy food only from merchants who had a "sacred book"—that is, from Christians and Jews, whose religions had a bible—but food purchased from Hindus could not be served at a Muslim table. The penalty for killing a non-Muslim was half that for killing a Muslim.[23]

As early as the beginning of the nineteenth century, there were Russian slaves in Bukhara. Some of them managed to buy their freedom from their Muslim masters and engage in trade or handicrafts, but even these relatively secure economic positions did not save them from Muslim contempt. The government of Bukhara used all means at its disposal to try to turn Russian Christians into Muslims. According to A.F. Middendorf, almost all Russian slaves were "forced into Islam, into wearing a turban and [being circumcised]."[24]

COMMUNIST RULE IN CENTRAL ASIA AND ITS RELATIONSHIP WITH LOCAL ISLAM

The disregard that Communist leaders had toward events in the Central Asian part of the Russian Empire after thei r 1917 seizure of power is illustrated by the telegram that Vladimir Lenin sent to his colleagues Eliava, Rudzutak, and Kuibyshev in Tashkent on December 11, 1919. It read as follows: "Your colleagues' demands are excessive. It is funny, or worse than funny, that you believe that Turkestan is more important than the Center and Ukraine."[25]

Those in Moscow, especially Stalin, did not want the people of Central Asia to be united within one Muslim Soviet state, so Turkestan was divided along ethnic linguistic lines into six states: the Uzbek and the Turkmen Soviet Socialist Republics (SSR), created in October 1924; the Tajik SSR, which went through several steps before being made a federal republic in October 1929; the Kirghiz and the Kazakh SSRs in December 1936; and the Karakalpak Autonomous Republic (within the Uzbek SSR), also in 1936.

But the Soviets did not destroy the ties and institutions that were blessed by Islam. Brute political force could not transform the traditional culture, the age-old way of life of the communities, and the semi-feudal economy, which was dominant for the majority of the population of Central Asia.

After the conquest of the independent Central Asian states, and the division of the region into Soviet Central Asian republics, the Communist leadership in Moscow for a long time had no interest in Islam *per se*, which they regarded as an ethnic holdover from the past; powerless, posing no political danger to the Center, and influencing the masses only in the sphere of family and marital relations.[26] And so Moscow delegated to the local party elites the responsibility for relating to Islam and the Muslim faithful.

The local Communists did not favor the breakup of the semi-feudal community structures and ties. While the Kremlin's long-range goals called for depriving the local farmers of the land, the local party elites were allowed to leave in place the traditional institutions of the peasants who were, after all, the majority of the population. Although these archaic ways were not responsive to communist ideology, they helped retard the political activities of the people, thus enabling the local rulers to amass unlimited political domination and turn the local peasants into obedient slaves on the cotton plantations.

According to Sergei Panarin, a Russian scholar of the East, the Moscow Center had no choice but to retain the Central Asian village in its traditional form. The Soviet cotton plantations, which occupied a major proportion of the fertile land in Central Asia, could not thrive without a workforce that had been raised to follow traditional community values of persistent and painstaking labor. Communist governors-general from Moscow (second secretaries of Central Asian party committees at various levels, from the republic committees to the district party committees) were interested only in ensuring that the local leadership remained loyal and that the republics fulfilled their economic, political, and military obligations towards the Center.

The Central Asian Communists knew that the problems related to Islam were far from insignificant. They knew that they could not leave unsupervised the important matter of regulating the religious behavior of the people. At the same time, the Communists clearly understood that their own image among the local population was that of infidels and usurpers—a situation that would make it difficult to establish direct contact with ordinary people, much less force

Muslims to abandon the spiritual culture of their everyday lives, which had been practiced over 11 centuries, for the sake of boring and incomprehensible Marxism-Leninism and Soviet-style pseudo-culture. Besides, a comparison of the Muslim past with the Soviet present clearly did not favor the latter.

As a first step to overcoming these problems, the local Communists created a new official Muslim clergy that could be counted on to carry out their political and ideological directives. It was to act as an intermediary between the elites' authority and the ordinary people, "building bridges" between the socialist and the Islamic doctrines. But the amount of independent influence official clergymen were allowed to have on the political life of the state changed dramatically from their relative freedom in Czarist days. They were barred from many of their former positions and lost not only independence in political behavior but also in purely religious matters. Their activities were put under the strict control of party committees, secret police administrations, the State Committee for Religious Affairs, and the Spiritual Administration of Muslims of Central Asia and Kazakhstan.

Despite the fact that these clergymen had little authority with their fellow countrymen because of their ties to the Communists, they were still viewed with a certain degree of respect because they had received a formal Muslim education in local *madrassas* and abroad, knew Arabic and could read the Qur'an, and—with the permission of local authorities—had gone on the Hajj to Saudi Arabia.

In any event, it was now their responsibility to devise ideological schemes to make socialist teachings and political practices understandable and acceptable to ordinary Muslims. They were to promulgate the idea that socialism was the only true unifying concept, that it did not contradict the basic principles of Islam, and that the socialist system was an organic part of Muslim society. Ideally, the official Muslim clergy were to convince ordinary Muslims that Soviet power had been established on earth by the will of Allah just as He had empowered the emirs and other secular authorities in the past. In essence, a Muslim was to accept socialism's inevitability and obey the Communists.

It was helpful that Islam, much like socialist doctrine, gives preference to the social group (the community, or ummah) over the individual. Both doctrines define an individual's value not by his personal qualities but by the extent of his usefulness to the community or collective. And, of course, both socialism and Islam demand unquestioning obedience from an individual.

Searching for other concordance between Marxist and Islamic doctrines, the official Muslim clergy, under the Communist politicians' strict control, proceeded to try to sell Marxism to the people of Central Asia. They portrayed the communist leaders of the proletarian revolution as evidence of the goodness of Allah, who "blessed" the world with Marx, Engels, and Lenin. The Uzbek Imam-hatib Sattarov, for example, described the creation of socialism as an act ordained by Allah:

> The oppressed and the exploited were searching for a way out of their painful situation. With the exception of Qur'anic teachings, however, no one could point the way to achieve this goal. No one could say how to wrest power from the hands of the bourgeoisie and landowners, how to liquidate private property in land and other means of production. There were people who knew the Qur'an and tried to tell people the truth. However, the wealthy, who used religion in their interests, ruined such people.

> Allah was not rushing, but He was doing His deed. The first ones in the history of humanity to answer these questions were Marx and Engels... Thus, for the first time in history, the theory of how to build socialism was developed. What remained was to do it in practice. So the omnipotent Allah raised a commander in the likeness of Marx and Engels. Allah passed the cause into the hands of our great commander, Lenin.[27]

This was entirely consonant with the Muslim model of a social system uniting state and spiritual power.

Islam and Marxism also defended the use of forcible methods to spread their teachings among those of a different faith: Islam glorifies holy war, *jihad*; Marxism-Leninism advocated a worldwide proletarian revolution. In the words of Imam Ahmedzian Mustafin:

> Social revolutions taking place in different countries bring about new forms of governing, and this is considered one of the basic principles

in Islam. History confirmed many times the validity of this Islamic principle and the tremendous importance of social revolutions for the progress of humanity. This can be seen in the example of the Great October Socialist Revolution, revolutions in Egypt, Yemen, Libya, and in many other countries.[28]

But official Islam also had to justify the actions of the Communists, among them seizing property from its legitimate owners. Although it was extremely difficult for the Muslim clergy to transform this criminal act to accord with Islamic teachings, they had to do so as early as the end of the 1920s. This statement was issued by the top Central Asian clergy in 1927:

> According to the teachings of the great Imam al-Ahzam, it is illegal and reprehensible to take harvest from the land and use it without personally engaging in agriculture, by leasing the land for planting to another person... The government has the right to confiscate the surplus of land from large landowners and distribute it to peasants who need land and are able to work it on their own.[29]

To prove to Turkmen peasants that the idea of creating *kolkhozes* (collective farms) had its origin in Islam, the official Muslim clerics in Turkmenistan used the legend from the national mythology about the spirit of Baba Daihan, the patron of farming. From time immemorial, Turkmen peasants planted a special field in his honor, the harvest from which became the property of all the members of the community. Part of this harvest was distributed to widows and orphans; another part was sold and the proceeds used to hold a common ritual meal. Later, this ancient communal custom became a part of Muslim religious rite, with prayers and other rituals, known as the *hudayi eli*. Referring to this rite, the official pro-Soviet theologians presented *kolkhoz* labor at cotton plantations as the "continuation of a good, old Muslim tradition."[30]

Community relations sanctified by Islam and preserved in their substance by long tradition, especially those in Central Asian villages, were assimilated and adopted by Soviet structures and institutions. For instance, *kolkhozes* and *sovkhozes* (state farms) were created on the basis of long-existing community boundaries. Within these collectives, the division into brigades and lots went along family and clan lines.

In their sermons, official pro-Soviet clerics impressed upon the faithful the thought that Soviet-style socialism was the societal model advocated by the Prophet Muhammad and that the Soviet state was building a paradise on earth for Muslims. The imam of the Khachmass Mosque, Agayev, addressed a Tashkent Muslim conference:

> I rejoice and bow before the genius of the Prophet, who had foreseen the social principles of socialism. I rejoice that many socialist customs are Prophet Muhammad's dream brought to life... The Holy Prophet showed the way to implement Islamic ideals. So now the people in our country live in freedom and prosperity, a life with a future, which is what the wise Prophet Muhammad was dreaming about.[31]

Kazi Kamal Bashirov, a Muslim judge, exhorted Muslims in 1970:

> There is nothing more important for our government than a man. It [our government] places all the national wealth at the service of the people. Our state wants to build a paradise on earth for you and me... Help the state in every way... in this noble cause, always keeping in mind that this is the most sacred duty of any faithful.[32]

Similarly, a former chairman of the Spiritual Administration of Muslims of Central Asia and Kazakhstan openly stated:

> The religion of Islam is an active supporter of building socialism and communism in our country. Concerns for the moral improvement of the people and guiding Muslims towards the road of Islam and socialism—this is what the Muslims' Administration, all the religious organizations' leaders in Central Asia and Kazakhstan, see as their main task.[33]

It should be noted that although the Central Asian Communists flirted with Islam and used the official clergy to try to meet their own political and ideological goals, they simultaneously spread vehement antireligious propaganda to impress Moscow and its emissaries. Voluminous reports on successes in atheistic work were sent to Moscow; local propaganda organs trumpeted their achievements in the struggle against Islam for the benefit of envoys from Moscow, knowing full well the duplicity of their grandiose claims.

From my own frequent personal contacts with members of the Central Asian party elite, however, I got the clear impression that in their relationships with Russians and other non-Muslims, Central Asian party bosses keenly felt their identification with the Muslim world and were hostile to all those of a different faith. In any event, they were familiar with the Muslim custom of *taqiyya*, according to which Muslims must conceal their true beliefs in front of those of a different faith. Moreover, a Muslim will be rewarded for deceiving an adherent of a different faith, since the norms of Muslim ethics do not extend to disbelievers. The custom of *taqiyya* permitted a Central Asian Communist to be duplicitous without feeling pangs of conscience. He could assure his Russian bosses of his adherence to atheism, while following Muslim customs in his family or while socializing with his compatriots.

THE SOVIET AUTHORITIES AND POPULAR ISLAM

As Alexandra Bennigsen and Marie Broxup have pointed out:

> Undoubtedly, "official Islam" is served by an extremely able "general staff" of well-trained *ulema*... On the other hand, it is difficult to imagine that... "official Islam" can meet even the minimum spiritual needs of Muslims. Clearly, another dimension is needed if the religion of the Prophet is to be preserved in the USSR.[34]

"Popular" Islam, the everyday religious practices of the people of Muslim faith, met these needs. Long entrenched in Central Asia, it combined Muslim dogma with a multitude of community customs, rites, and celebrations that originated in pre-Islamic times and passed through the generations virtually unchanged. A Muslim true to his faith strictly observed the ancient traditions; anyone questioning, much less doubting, the accepted ways was guilty of heresy and severely censured. These traditions of faith had stood the test of time and had not given way to those who might have wanted to change them, because they satisfied the spiritual needs of the people.

Everyday Islam in Central Asia was independent of official Islam and parallel to it, not needing the pro-Soviet official clergy to guide the religious behavior of the people because Muslim believers allow any member of the faithful who knows the basic dogma and rites to head the community. Most of these individuals had regular jobs in the national economy. It has only been a recent development that Muslim clerics might spend their lives as professionals.[35]

The civil rites instituted by the communist leadership did not compete in any fundamental way with the rites of traditional Muslim life: for instance, Soviet law required that marriages, births, and deaths be recorded locally. The Muslims complied, but only because they wanted to live in the state legally. For the community, however, a marriage was considered valid only if it was blessed by an imam. The imam was present at the birth of a baby; his sacred duties included taking part in naming the infant and in circumcising newborn boys. And it was completely unthinkable to bury a deceased Muslim without an imam to perform the *janazah*, the religious burial service.

The Central Asian party elites acknowledged the strength and influence of popular Islam by demonstrating their adherence to ethnic traditions and Muslim commandments when dealing with ordinary people. This was pragmatism in action, showing their fellow countrymen that they too were sincere champions of Islam and that, implicitly, their position at the helm of power was sanctioned by Allah's will.

For the Central Asian *nomenklatura* (state elite), the task of establishing relations with popular Islam and utilizing its norms and values became a matter of professional importance. The *nomenklatura* ran the administrative affairs of the state, including responsibility for managing state industrial enterprises, kolkhozes and sovkhozes, the official trade sector, and all other state institutions. These administrators had control over all the daily economic activities of ordinary people, making them almost totally dependent on the state.

Central Asian functionaries raised under the Soviet regime and compelled to become CPSU members to get their jobs might have had to publicly proclaim themselves atheists and even participate in official antireligious campaigns for Moscow's benefit, but in their everyday lives they followed Islamic traditions, treated the national cultural legacies with respect, and revered their parents' past. As Bennigsen and Broxup observed: "They may be Sovietized on the surface, but they remain nationalists and Muslims."[36] As a result of this schizophrenic process, the Central Asian communist officials became very skilled in the use of

Islamic principles governing relations between power holders and subordinates for the purpose of strengthening their own power.

In carrying out his functions as a "boss" in his contacts with ordinary people, a *nomenklatura* manager did not need to don the garb of the true Communist who represented proletarian power. After all, even in the consciousness of the most modern generation of Central Asian Muslims, this power was not seen to have been sanctioned by Allah. It was much better for a state functionary to present himself as a true Muslim, knowledgeable about the Qur'an and Shari'ah, discharging his responsibilities in power in accordance with Islamic dogma. This permitted him to gain the allegiance of his subordinates and others dependent on him, which in turn made it possible for him to operate following local customs rather than Soviet law—a situation that was ideally suited for bribe-taking. Under the Soviet system, this was the main source of functionaries' incomes.

Thus, corruption flourished within the circles of the Central Asian *nomenklatura*; it became a normal feature of the local socioeconomic system. Corruption helped Central Asian functionaries easily come to an understanding with Moscow, receive multimillion-ruble subsidies for the development of their republics, and divide those subsidies among themselves, even sharing some of them with ordinary people. As James Critchlow, a fellow at the Russian Research Center of Harvard University, correctly noted, "[w]hen one takes a close look at the corruption in the Central Asian republics from the standpoint of local public interests, it resembles not so much an abstract evil as a mixture of positive and negative components."[37]

According to Michael Rywkin, corruption in Central Asia provided "social stability in the region."[38] In fact, in the environment of the super centralized Soviet economy, with hundreds of directives originating in Moscow and the local bureaucracies—often contradicting one another—problems could be resolved in many cases only on a practical, common-sense basis, while circumventing the law. Such solutions, however, inevitably depended on the approval of a functionary, which could be obtained only through a bribe. At the same time, the informal norms of relations between people, sanctified by the authority of Islam, made both giving and taking bribes easier.

We can conclude that in addition to the specific features of Islam as a religion, the tenacity of popular, everyday Islam in Central Asia during the Soviet years was due to the fact that the local *nomenklatura* had a stake in perpetuating it. Popular Islam and ancient Muslim traditions, which sanctified the power of the secular authorities and afforded them ample opportunity for enrichment, ensured the stability of the *nomenklatura*'s power and provided it with the continuous ability to exchange favors for material remuneration from ordinary people. As Riyaz Masalim noted, "the durability of power in Muslim republics [of the former Soviet Union] stems not from the rudiments of communist totalitarianism but first and foremost from the traditions of authoritarianism and deep respect for the supreme ruler inherent in a Muslim society."[39]

ISLAM AND THE SOVIET CAMPAIGN TO SPREAD SOCIALISM

Until the beginning of the 1960s, Moscow did not pay close attention to official Muslim theologians and clerics, considering relations with them to be the exclusive province of the Central Asian party elite. This situation began to change when young nations, the former colonies of European countries, started to become independent members of the international community. Some of the leaders of these new nations began to proclaim their allegiance to socialist ideas and their desire to import socialism for their people. Among these countries were quite a few with predominantly Muslim populations (the Arab countries, some states in sub-Saharan Africa, Indonesia, Bangladesh, and others). As in Central Asia, leaders of these Muslim countries had to reconcile the ideals of Islam with socialist programs of reorganization they wanted to promote.

The advent of such states inspired new hope in the hearts of the Kremlin leaders. By that time, they had begun to realize that the Soviet socialist model had practically no prospects for attracting the sympathies of a majority of the population in Western countries and that a proletarian revolution in the West did not have a serious chance of succeeding. Soviet ideologues heard the leaders of the new African and Asian nations condemn Western colonialism along with capitalism and imperialism and thought they saw possibilities for the implementation of their revolutionary ideals.

Under Khrushchev, the Soviet state rushed to undertake huge economic projects in Third World countries whose leaders were gravitating to socialism. The Soviets invested enormous amounts of money in projects such as the Aswan High Dam in Egypt and metallurgical plants in India in their eagerness to promote the ideological goals of the proletarian revolution in the Third World.

But more than just economic and political aid was needed to bring the Muslim leaders of the young independent states into the Soviet orbit of influence. They had to be persuaded of the attractiveness of the Soviet socialist model and impressed by a positive image of the Soviet Union. Creating such an image abroad became a major propaganda task for Soviet ideologues, whose objective was to contrast the alleged superiority of Soviet socialism with the presumed bankruptcy of capitalism.

This effort went on for years and encompassed Soviet mass communications aimed at foreign audiences, propaganda and political influence campaigns in other Islamic countries, activities of the cultural centers of Soviet embassies and Soviet friendship societies abroad, all organized and directed by the Communist Party Central Committee's Ideology Department in collaboration with the Central Committee's International Department. The Central Committee or its mediators briefed Soviet professional, scientific, cultural, and youth delegations traveling to foreign countries on how to act and what to say abroad in order to do their part to foster the correct portrait of the Soviet Union, an image of great importance to the party elite.

The Soviets did their best to convert their new Middle Eastern friends into champions of a political system that enabled a small group of politically influential people to wield power over the entire nation. It was a very attractive idea to military officers or businessmen from Islamic states who went to the USSR to study Soviet arms manuals or do business with Soviet oil companies.

In their worldwide ideological campaign to ingratiate themselves with Islamic countries, Soviet leaders took as their basic premise that the ideas and beliefs of Muslims were powerful forces that could not be denied and had to be taken into account as they crafted strategies for persuasion. Soviet ideological workers were not to try to change the religious beliefs of Muslims but were to set them to one side and emphasize the secular aspects of Muslim life.

The Soviets understood that the belief in Allah is very strong, so their position when addressing a Muslim audience was that socialism was concerned with science, with facts here on earth, and not with religious beliefs. The question of whether God exists was not a scientific issue and therefore was not of concern to communism. If Muslims wished to believe in Allah, that was their business and Marxism had nothing against it. Soviet propaganda aimed at the Muslim world studiously avoided mentioning the fact that the Soviet Union was an atheistic state.

In fact, Soviet propagandists even portrayed the Soviet Union as being a Muslim country, at least in part because of the fact that tens of millions of Muslims lived there. They stressed that the Soviet state respected believers and that it repaired mosques and built new ones. This last point was true because in their effort to fight the underground Islamic movement, Soviet authorities had stepped up their utilization of the official Muslim clergy. They were building new mosques and repairing others to draw the Muslim people into the official religious network.

For foreign audiences, Soviet propagandists claimed that the renewed encouragement of Islam in the USSR demonstrated Soviet respect for the rights of believers, and they pointed out that the Soviet authorities were publishing Muslim magazines, opening new Islamic schools, talking with Saudi Arabia about opening a center for Islamic study there, and so on. They stressed those facts that could be made to fit the theme that Islam was alive, well, and even prospering in the Soviet Union. At the same time, Soviet-sanctioned official mullahs and muftis continuously visited the Persian Gulf states with good will messages from the Soviet government, urging them to develop various kinds of relationships with the USSR.

But presenting the Soviet state as the best friend of Islam and Muslims everywhere was not entirely the spiritual exercise it appeared to be; rather, it was a pragmatic and material attempt to gain access to the wealthy fundamentalist states and their hard currency in order to finance projects that would help relieve the agony of the Soviet economy. When oil prices declined sharply in the mid-1980s, the Soviets had to look somewhere to make up their losses.

The Iran-Iraq war gave Soviet policymakers a very profitable revenue source: massive arms sales to the combatants—both Iran and Iraq. Access to Middle

East arms markets may also have helped the Soviets disseminate the Communist political example of establishing a one-party regime—even to Third World countries that did not accept Marxist ideology. Many times, I heard

Syrian and Iraqi Ba'athists tell Soviet representatives that they had used the CPSU example in building the Ba'ath Party and had found that it worked very well.

The Soviets' approaches to Islam outside Central Asia sometimes brought the unexpected: in February 1989, Soviet Foreign Minister Eduard Shevardnadze traveled extensively to meet with leaders of Muslim states and was received in Iran by the Ayatollah Khomeini himself, who later went so far as to personally issue an invitation to Gorbachev to embrace Islam.

ISLAMIC THREATS TO COMMUNIST RULE

Notwithstanding that in Soviet times the presence of Islam in the Central Asian republics had been used as a tool to solidify relationships with Middle Eastern and other Islamic countries, and the Brezhnev "era of stagnation" had allowed an almost "live and let live" policy to exist relative to domestic Islamic activities in the republics, after Yuri Andropov became general secretary of the Communist Party of the Soviet Union, the Communists' attitude about Islam underwent significant change. Andropov had been head of the KGB. During inquiries about corruption in Uzbekistan, Kazakhstan, and Azerbaijan that he carried out in the early 1980s, it became clear to the KGB and the top party elites in Moscow that Islam was very much alive in these regions, and it began to be seen as one of the major political opponents and rivals to communist rule at the all-union and local levels. They feared Islam's strong influence on the faithful and its ability to organize the activities of the Soviet Muslim masses.

Andropov launched an anti-Muslim campaign that, by the time Mikhail Gorbachev became leader, resulted in 26,000 officials in Islamic regions being fired, fined, or disciplined for incompetence and corruption. The government's anti-Islamic policy increased in tempo under Gorbachev. In November 1986, he met with members of the Central Committee of the Uzbek Communist Party. Gorbachev expressed so much hostility toward Islam in his instructions to local Communists that his speech was not reported in major Soviet newspapers.

Only the local newspaper *Pravda Vostoka* informed the Muslim population that Gorbachev had "declared an uncompromising battle" against domestic Islam and ordered an increase in political activities and atheistic propaganda against it.[40]

Given his general attempts to improve relations with religious organizations, especially the Russian Orthodox Church, this stance may seem contradictory, but Gorbachev—and others in power—blamed Islam for organized resistance to Soviet rule. Further, he believed that because Muslims proclaimed loyalty to Islam, they could not as well be loyal to the communist community called the "Soviet people."

One can state with certainty that when Gorbachev took office he did not consider the nationalities issue—as he understood it—to be a serious problem. Notwithstanding other events, in his 1987 book, *Perestroika: New Thinking for Our Country and the World*, Gorbachev reiterated all the ideological clichés about how the Union of Soviet Socialist Republics was a paradise for diverse nationalities:

> Czarist Russia was called a prison of nations. The Revolution and socialism have done away with national oppression and inequality and ensured economic, intellectual, and cultural progress for all nations and nationalities. Formerly backward nations have acquired advanced industry and a modern social structure. Our Party has carried out a tremendous amount of work and has transformed the situation. Its results have enriched Soviet society and world civilization in general.[41]

Gorbachev acknowledged that "it sometimes happens that, in the process, a certain section of people descend to nationalism. Narrow nationalist views, national rivalry, and arrogance emerge." But the Soviet leader said these "negative phenomena" were the result of bureaucratic "red tape" and complained that there were "quite a few people in the West and, for that matter, in the East who would like to undermine the friendship and cohesion of the peoples of the Soviet Union." In the spirit of the old Stalinist national policy, Gorbachev then threatened nationalists, saying, "Soviet law stands on guard, protecting the accomplishments of the Leninist nationality policy."[42]

Before the ink could dry on Gorbachev's manuscript, national movements had blossomed throughout the Soviet Union: in the Baltic States and Central Asia, in Moldova and Ukraine, in Georgia, Armenia, and Azerbaijan, and even in the Russian Republic itself. These movements were not made up of "a certain section of people" with "narrow nationalist views" who happened to "descend to nationalism," but of Muslims in Azerbaijan, Tajikistan, and the Fergana Valley who armed themselves in order to fight the oppressive local party committees and police. The disintegration of the Soviet empire became an immediate danger.

The drive for independence in the Soviet Muslim republics had deep roots in their national heritage, but it was a religious heritage, not a civic one, and this was what Gorbachev failed to understand. Islam in these regions was not merely a set of pure religious beliefs but rather an active ideology, a lifestyle molding all Soviet Muslims. Islamic dogma about the linking of social and governmental life set the standard for many aspects of social, political, and even economic life in the "socialist society" of the Soviet Muslim republics.

In 1983, Alexandre Bennigsen and Marie Broxup had predicted:

> The role of radically conservative Muslims in the USSR is not limited just to the preservation of religious believers, and Sufi *tariqa* are not concerned merely with cult observation. In Islam, the religious, national, and political spheres are tightly interwoven, and consequently the Sufi brotherhood have [sic] become the focal point of traditional opposition to the Russian presence. For the present, the Sufi orders remain traditionalist, closed societies believing that only religion can constitute the proper basis of the unity of the Muslim *ummah*, "the community of the believers." However, since the war [in Afghanistan], some orders have become more and more infused with nationalism, with the result that any nationalist movement—even progressive—which is bound to emerge will be strongly influenced by the traditionalist conservative ideas of Sufism.[43]

This prediction turned out to be correct. Muslims in the USSR always defended their religion and traditions in terms of nationalism. The Soviet authorities, however, responded that Islam (and its associated underground community) represented a threat to the Soviet system and characterized their repression of it in terms of a struggle against nationalism and chauvinism.

THE REPUBLICS BREAK AWAY

Gorbachev's policies of *glasnost* (openness) and *perestroika* (restructuring) essentially destroyed the official ideology of the Soviet state and the ruling communist party elite. The ideology of Marxism-Leninism, after holding sway over the minds and deeds of the Soviet people for seven decades, finally proved to be totally fruitless. The critique of Marxism-Leninism as a program for guiding concrete activities, launched with the start of *perestroika*, stigmatized the ideology that had provided the ultimate justification for the interests of party functionaries.

Several years of *glasnost* and the dissemination of free publications exposed the criminal past of the Soviet government as well as that of the Communist Party, including not only its leaders in the Central Committee but also those in the republic and regional party committees. Such disclosures rid people of their previous illusions concerning the "noble aims" of the Communists, in both the past and at that time. This situation was used by national popular fronts, which headed movements for secession and contributed greatly to the drive for separation that developed in different republics and regions of the USSR. These fronts started to attack not only the central Soviet government but also communist parties in the republics and local communist leaders.

In promoting the policies of *glasnost* and *perestroika*, Mikhail Gorbachev had certainly never expected to engender such widespread change so fast, particularly his own loss of office. Openness (relaxing restrictions the people were increasingly restive about) and restructuring (as long as the Communist Party remained the foundation of the edifice) seemed safe enough gambits to defuse some of the tensions rampant in the union and even bring about some sorely needed economic improvement.

At the heart of the process, however, was the local party elites' fierce desire to be rid of the overarching authority of the Central Committee of the CPSU. This was not a new phenomenon but long-endured aggravation, despite the considerable power they wielded themselves. (This was amply demonstrated as far back as 1963, when Nikita Khrushchev attempted to take their activities under his control. Within a year, he was ousted from all of his positions in the party and the government. Since that time, none of the CPSU general secretaries dared to defy the will of the local party elites.)

Perestroika's economic strategy was to privatize state property and thus give greater opportunities to the private sector. The local party elites recognized the efficiency of the private sector's business activities; moreover, they were dependent for the greater part of their incomes on bribes they received from the shadow economy, so they hoped *perestroika* would leave political power in their hands, albeit under a different banner, and at the same time increase their wealth and improve their standard of living by providing even more sources of kickbacks.

The *nomenklatura* officials who controlled Soviet state property were not happy with this turn of events. They began to resist the party bosses and sabotage the new directives to implement radical economic reforms. Because the *nomenklatura* made up the vast majority of rank-and-file party members, their refusal to go along with the privatization of state property forced the local party elites to bolt from the party. Beginning in the summer of 1988, they left the party structures and moved into new government organizations or into the private sector. In the process, they concealed abroad or invested in local private businesses billions of dollars and rubles from the national and party coffers.

Things came to a head in August 1991, when a number of the higher-ranking *nomenklatura* officials, along with old-guard Kremlin Communists who favored a centralized Soviet Union, attempted a coup in Moscow. The effort failed because they had not prepared adequately and they found little support for their cause. (There are those who say that the dissidents were provoked into rebellion by Yeltsin and his team of local party elites.) Nonetheless, the fact that a coup had been instigated gave Yeltsin the opportunity to decree the end of the Communist Party, and the blocks began to tumble. By December, all of the republics had broken away; the union had disintegrated.

The *nomenklatura* at the republic level kept their jobs. This group actually gained strength, and its membership grew as some of the party elites from the newly banned party committees joined its forces. The political role of this expanded *nomenklatura* also became more powerful when the party committees that had previously controlled their careers disappeared.

As the facade of Marxism-Leninism crumbled, Soviet party functionaries, including those in the Central Asian republics, began to cast about for a new ideology so that they could, once again, portray themselves as the true advocates of the people's interests and legitimize their right to power. In truth, the Russian (as well as the Kazakh, Kyrgyz, Uzbek, and all other) representatives of the *nomenklatura* were only concerned with one problem: how to maintain their own wealth and comfort.

Despite the disintegration of the Soviet Union, the destruction of the credibility of Marxist-Leninist theories, and the ban on the activities of communist parties in the majority of Central Asian states, most of the essential features of the political system created by the Communists have endured. The best evidence of this is that, except in Kyrgyzstan, Communists remain in power as the heads of their countries, and the local apparatus of the former Communist Party still controls most of the political and economic power in their regimes. These officials are deftly using their positions of authority to block all serious sociopolitical and economic reforms.

The immutable factor is the preservation of the party elites' self-serving interests; however, it has become necessary to clothe their interests in the terminology of another social theory in order to repudiate communism and to present their interests as universal, justifying their hold on power. They have cynically embraced social-democratic and national-liberal slogans, but for the most part they have seen the pragmatic wisdom of declaring themselves to be genuine defenders of Islam, not just in their everyday lives and in their interpersonal relationships, as they had done in the past, but also publicly, on the official level, in their bid to stay in leadership positions. It is obvious that they will do just about anything to keep their privileged positions and continue to enjoy all the benefits that a Communist-style regime bestows on those at the top. The former Communists may have abandoned communist ideology but not their love of power.

COMMUNISTS IN ISLAMIC CLOTHING

Central Asian communists understood very well that the structure of Central Asian society underwent certain changes during the Soviet period, but the Muslim way of life was not altered drastically. The affiliation of the majority of the clergy and religious believers with the Communist Party had been purely a ormality attributable to foreign pressure. The Communist Party as an institution had been essential for—and actively used by—the CPSU leadership alone.

Islam influenced the sociopolitical situation in Central Asia despite efforts by Moscow to suppress or tame Islamic religious behavior. Having acquired independence from Moscow—from the Central Committee of the CPSU and the all-union ministries' *nomenklatura*—the Central Asian party elites became even stronger when they officially abandoned communist ideology and openly embraced Islamic ideas, laws, and methods of reinforcing their authority. They were able to do this rather competently, since the Central Asian communist officials even during Soviet times were very skilled in the use of Islamic dogmas for strengthening their own power.

To demonstrate to the Muslim masses their new image and their break with the communist past, the party elites in some republics, together with the local *nomenklatura*, renamed the local communist parties, making an effort to establish an aura more in tune with the times. The Uzbek Communist Party, for instance, became the People's Democratic Party of Uzbekistan; the Kazakh Communist Party is now called the Socialist Party; the Communists who had left the Tajik Communist Party joined the ranks of the United Democratic Party of Tajikistan; the Turkmen Communist Party took a long time to come up with a new name, but it changed to the Democratic Party in 1992. In Kyrgyzstan alone—the only Central Asian republic where a man who had no relation to the Communist Party elite (Askar Akayev) was elected as the republic's first president—did the local Communist Party cease to exist.

Despite the fact that they changed the names of their parties, the neo-Communists have not discarded the party structures they had used in the past to hold all power in their own hands. As a justification for their power, however, they look to (and find backing in) the principles of Islam. All of them have recognized Islam as a state religion, but they work only with the obedient official clergy. Official ecclesiastics have become deputies in national parliaments and other state organs, but the independent clergy and members of the Islamic revival movement (especially fundamentalists) are still as severely persecuted as they were during the Brezhnev era of stagnation.

All of the new Central Asian presidents took the oath of office by placing their hand on the Qur'an, and they have become regular visitors to mosques during Muslim holidays. At their initiative, state symbols have acquired Islamic features:

national flags are now green and carry the Islamic crescent moon, and new state seals display ornamental Arabic script.

Not limiting themselves to such symbolic demonstrations of their ideological makeover, the Central Asian neo-Communists work to portray themselves as Islamic democrats who trust the people and draw on Islamic traditions in administering state power. And, to burnish their credentials as the champions of Islam, Central Asia's local leaders opened their doors to Saudi Wahhabis who, in the beginning of 1990s, came to the newly independent Central Asian states under the pretext of building mosques and supplying Qur'ans.

According to Shamshibek Shakirovich Zakirov, adviser to the chairman of the State Commission on Religious Affairs in the Osh region of the Republic of Kyrgyzstan, who has worked in governmental bodies that control religious institutions for 20 years, ten mosques were constructed in the city of Osh alone after 1990 as a result of assistance from Saudi Arabia, which financed that construction and provided Wahhabi literature in local languages for these mosques.[44] Habibulla hajji Zalikhaev, head of a *madrassa* in Dargin settlement no. 20 in Kyrgyzstan, told me during our meeting in August 2004:

> When Arabs from Saudi Arabia came to us, they said: "We shall help you with money to build mosques." When these Arabs were about to complete construction of the Central Mosque in Bishkek, they told us: "As soon as we end construction of the mosque, we shall bring our imam to work in this mosque" Our then chief mufti Kimsanbai hajji Abdurakhmanov asked them: "Why do you want to appoint your imam to us?" They answered: "Because we helped you to build the mosque." Kimsanbai hajji said: "Be so kind as to help us to build mosques, but it is for the chief mufti of KR to nominate their imams." Then they told him that they would discontinue building that mosque.[45]

Very soon, the local leaders discovered that Wahhabis were promoting their own ideology, which encouraged local opposition forces to support an Islamic caliphate rather than the local, post-Soviet governments. For instance, the government of the Kyrgyz Republic expressed its official concern that in the Fergana valley in the early 1990s:

[the] numbers of illegal private religious schools increased… and their contacts with foreign [Saudi] Muslim organizations expanded. As a result of such contacts not only the functioning character of these centers, but also their ideology had changed. Those schools of traditional Islamic education turned into independent radical religious centers the program of which, except for training, included propagation of their own social and political views.[46]

The local authorities challenged the Wahhabis in their own way. Zakirov told me:

In the early 1990s, we understood that the ideas of radical Islam come to us from Saudi Arabia, through our youth who studied abroad and through our Muslims who performed the Hajj to Saudi Arabia. We followed the situation very closely and thought carefully about measures that we had to undertake against Wahhabis. We stated that Hizb ut-Tahrir members had no right to criticize our government. We told them, "Do you want freedom for Islam? You have it, since our fundamental laws protect believers. Do you want to build a mosque? Please, do it: there are no restrictions on such activities. Do you want to go to a mosque? It is also allowed. Do you want to study in a *madrassa*? Please, do it: there are no restrictions. We have no restrictions on religious freedoms. Then, from whom do you want to liberate Islam? We want our population to have immunity against ideas of extremists. Our authorities explain to our population, to believers, to clergy, that it is harmful to politicize Islam.[47]

Habibulla hajji Zalikhaev believes:

We need personnel that know and understand Islam, the staff who could stop the movements of radical Islam. They should be able to lead a dialogue without scandal, without weapons, by diplomatic ways. It is necessary to train local experts who know what the terms "jihad" and "Sufism" mean. "Jihad" is not a military action, but the self-effort of a Muslim to reach better understanding of Islam. Representatives of Hizb ut-Tahrir would tell us that the world was divided into "an area of war" where today's Muslim countries are located, and "an area of peace"—where the caliphate located. But since no caliphate exists in this world today, Hizb ut-Tahrir opposes the entire world; the whole world is "an area of war." We tell them: "Listen, it was like this in the

7th Century, when there was a war against our Prophet. His enemies wanted to kill him, to be at war with him. At that time, perhaps, such a division of the world into two areas was correct, but now times had changed and there is no such division today.[48]

According to Dr. Orozbek Moldaliev, one of the top experts on Islamic terrorism from the Bishkek Diplomatic Academy, the mutual enmity between communists and both the Saudi-backed Wahhabis and the radical Islamist party of Hizb ut-Tahrir may be explained by great similarity between these two groups. Dr. Orozbek Moldaliev believes that both groups have a utopian ultimate goal: in the first case, world communism, in the second, a world caliphate. Both parties dislike real democracy and seek to establish a mythical perfect society. Both groups rely on internationalism and illegal activities, and seek to change people's consciousness by means of propaganda.

The threat of Wahhabism to the very existence of civil society has also been discovered by "civilized" opposition. According to Dr.Yuri Kulchik, by the early 1990s both the establishment and the "civilized" opposition understood that the question was not one of "a trivial reshuffling of power, but rather a truly radical revolution" if Wahhabism were to replace the national secular elite: "The national intelligentsia would undoubtedly fall prey to a radical Islamization of public life. The secular, atheistic and 'Europeanized' elite would be unable to fit into an Islamic model of development. Iranian and Taliban examples leave no room for illusions." That is why Central Asian national intellectuals supported local leaders "whenever fundamentalist Islam reared its head."[49]

Wahhabism challenged the new "Islamic" ideology of local ruling elites and threatened their power positions by encouraging the Muslim clergy and members of fundamentalist parties and organizations to assume state power. In the early 1990s, the Wahhabis in Central Asia had been gaining political strength and public influence. It was during this same period that various Islamic fundamentalist parties and organizations emerged, with membership numbering in the tens of thousands. For instance, in November 1991, the Islamic Revival Party was legalized in Tajikistan, although it has never been officially registered. In early 1992, the Alash fundamentalist party began to operate actively in Kazakhstan. And in the winter of 1992, Uzbek President Islam Karimov attempted to organize negotiations with Adolat, an opposition organization that considers itself fundamentalist. Sadykjan-haji, head of Kyrgyzstan's Islamic

Center, explained the fundamentalist views of such movements: "While their methods and strategies may differ, almost all of the groups listed above have as a shared goal the overthrow of the secular government and society and the establishment of an Islamic state, typically a caliphate."[50]

Thus, long before September 11, Central Asian governments recognized the danger posed by radical Islamists. In response, these governments embarked upon a series of important steps to de-legitimize the ideology of Wahhabism, to limit its ideological influence on local Muslims, and to inculcate immunity to Wahhabism in the hearts and minds of local youth in order to prevent them from joining radical Islamist organizations and terrorist groups. For example, the Central Asian governments, especially those in Uzbekistan and Kyrgyzstan, have created and developed an educational system—from kindergarten up to the university level—that inculcates the moral norms and social principles of tolerant Islam, and that respects the value of any human life (Muslim, Christian, Jewish, or other). The system provides textbooks for schools, cartoons for children, education for imams of local mosques, a network of counselors in Islamic affairs for central and local administrations, and television and radio talk shows that challenge the Wahhabi interpretation of the Qur'an and hadiths and provide listeners with a vision of tolerant Islam. They have created a network of educational establishments and research centers for schools and colleges that champion the tolerant and peaceful ideas of Islam and condemn Wahhabi ideas. Students of *madrassas* and universities in Tashkent and Bishkek study Arabic intensively, and upon graduation can not only read and interpret the Qur'an and hadiths, but also teach in Arabic. Graduates of these educational establishments become knowledgeable imams for mosques and theology teachers for public schools.

The Central Asian governments rely on the support of local Muslim scholars who advocate tolerant Islam. Scholars such as Dr. Abdujabar A. Abduvakhitov, rector of the Westminster International University in Tashkent, have argued that the whole body of radical Islamists should be divided into two parts: supporters of Wahhabi ideas and terrorists. While the "supporters" compose a rather numerous group (about 255,000 in Uzbekistan), the terrorist cells consist of 5-15 members (totaling perhaps about 100-150 in Uzbekistan) who not only share the ideas of Wahhabism, but are ready to commit terrorist acts and even sacrifice their own lives. The terrorist cells are only the tip of the iceberg, while the "supporters" are its body. Fighting terrorist cells is a mission of law enforcement agencies. It is practically impossible to re-educate these fanatics. According to Dr. Abduvakhitov, the mission of state educational establishments is to influence the mass group of "supporters" of Wahhabism, and—even more important—to educate young Muslims in the spirit of traditional, tolerant Central Asian Islam. The "battle of ideas" with Wahhabism should prevent "supporters" from becoming terrorists, and inoculate young people's minds against Wahhabi ideology.[51]

Dr. Zukhriddin Munimovich Khusnidinov, who has served as rector of the Islamic University since 1999 and State Councilor to the President of the Republic of Uzbekistan since 1998, believes that radical Islamists do not understand the essence of Islam. He believes the pretense of Central Asian Wahhabis to be experts in Qur'an and the hadiths only is effective because the majority of the Central Asian population has no profound knowledge of original Islam due to the restrictions that existed during Soviet times. He sincerely believes that it is very important to educate youth and give young people a proper understanding of Islamic principles and their implementation in real life. He says the challenge posed by the Wahhabis should be met by activities of the Islamic University and the mass media, especially radio and television broadcasting. Tashkent Islamic University does its best to insert proper Islamic studies into the existing curricula of schools, colleges and universities. The Islamic University supervises working teams that prepare textbooks for educational establishments at all levels. The teams include experts in Islamic law, in state law, in pedagogic sciences, and in sociology as well as representatives of the government. The teams select educational establishments in different regions of the country to test the system before introducing it on the total national level. The Islamic University has its own television studio where students prepare programs on Islamic issues for local television, and these programs are very popular on state and private channels.[52]

According to Dr. Asanov Avazbek, the Dean of the Theology Department at the Osh State University of Kyrgyzstan, Wahhabis who were trained in Saudi Arabia conduct propaganda work among the Kyrgyz population. Wahhabis and supporters of Hizb ut-Tahrir are engaged in ideological work, and the measures of law enforcement units against ideology will not help. Dr. Asanov says: "Against ideology it is necessary to struggle with the help of another ideology. For example, it not difficult ideologically to prove, that the goal of

Wahhabis and Hizb ut-Tahrir to create a caliphate in Central Asia is not a real one. One has just to explain in plain words for ordinary people that there is no caliphate even in Arab countries. So, how can one be established in the Kyrgyz Republic?"[53]

The U.S. policy community should study the arguments that such scholars and clerics have developed in places such as the Central Asian republics. As moderate Muslims, Central Asians have developed ways to counter Wahhabi ideology that rely on the traditions and concepts of local, tolerant Islam. Most Central Asian Muslims are "Bukhara" champions of Islam, who are much older and have much more authority within the Islamic world than advocates of Wahhabism. Their quarrel with Wahhabism is based on a very precise knowledge of the Qur'an and hadiths, the sayings of the Prophet—a type of knowledge that is very rare among Western experts.

American politicians and journalists should, at a minimum, be aware of the Central Asian Muslims' critique of Wahhabism and, whenever possible and appropriate, employ their language, arguments, discussion methods, theological sources, images, allegories, examples, and so on. Such an analysis is likely to contribute to defeating the advocates of Wahhabism on their own turf— the knowledge of original Islamic ideas—thereby hopefully weakening or demolishing their distorted vision of Islam and demonstrating that this extremist ideology is at odds with mainstream Islam. By examining how Central Asians fight Wahhabism and its Saudi supporters, Americans can better understand how to shape effective aid programs in key Muslim regions in order to make moderate Muslims more successful, and to give Muslim opponents of militant Islamism a more powerful voice than that which they currently have.

THE WAHHABI OUTLOOK AND ITS ADVOCATES

Wahhabism is an extremist political ideology, which uses the language of Islamic theology—or, more precisely, certain provisions of the Qur'an and Sunnah (the sayings and deeds of the Prophet Muhammad), as well as selected terms and ideas of Fascism and Bolshevism—in order to put forth an agenda of contemporary anti-Westernism and anti-Americanism, which we shall refer to as "fanatical anti-Americanism."

THE HISTORICAL ROOTS OF WAHHABISM

The Wahhabi doctrine was established by Muhammad ibn 'Abd al-Wahhab. He was born in Uyaynah in the Arabian region of Najd in 1703 and died in 1792. For many years, he engaged in commerce in modern-day Iraq, Iran, and Syria. In Baghdad, he married an affluent woman whose property he inherited when she died. Moving to Iran, he began to teach there. On returning to his native city, he wrote *Kitab at-tauhid* ("The Book of Monotheism"), which is the main text for Wahhabi doctrines. His followers call themselves al-muwahhidun, or "monotheists." The term Wahhabi is generally used by non-Muslims and opponents.

In 1744, 'Abd al-Wahhab was exiled from his native city because of his controversial preaching and the teachings in his book. He sought protection from Muhammad ibn Saud, the ruler of the town and surrounding area of Ad-Dir'iyah. Protection was granted, and this became the basis for an alliance that endures today among the followers of both men. The Saudi sheikh was impressed with 'Abd al-Wahhab and used his condemnation of other Muslims as polytheists as a pretext for waging what he termed holy war—*jihad*—against his neighbors. By 1811, the al-Saud family, allied with the Wahhabis, ruled over all the lands of Arabia, except for Yemen, from their new capital, Riyadh. Their alliance was strengthened by the wedding of ibn Saud's son to 'Abd al-Wahhab's daughter. Ibn Saud used the ideology of Wahhabism in his effort to subdue other tribes in the Arabian peninsula. Religion proved to be the most potent force for motivating disparate tribesmen.

The Ottoman sultan, with help from the Egyptians, drove the Saudis/Wahhabis from power for a time in the early 1800s, but they reassembled their power and established the second Saudi state from 1824 to 1891, before again being driven from power. The third triumph for the Wahhabi movement came when Abd al-Aziz al Saud captured Riyadh in 1902. By 1932, his control had expanded to nearly all of his ancestral domain. The state was named Saudi Arabia, where Wahhabism remains dominant to this day.

Since the establishment of the first Saudi state, the Wahhabi clergy have created a strong ideological institution that sanctified the political power of the Saudi royal family and justified the political and economic system it created. In return, the Wahhabi clerics enjoyed permanent financial support from the Saudi Arabian government. Wahhabism became the internal ideology of the Saudi ruling political class, which, before the 1980s, did not pretend to play a significant role in world political or economic affairs.

Things changed dramatically in the 1980s, when Wahhabi clergy, with the help of the Saudi government, began and preaching hatred against the United States and its allies and disseminating Wahhabi ideology among Muslims all over the world. Over the past 20 years, the Saudis have spent approximately $87 billion[54] to publish textbooks and shape school curricula, to install their own brand of Islamic experts in major Muslim universities and cultural centers, in an effort to make Muslims believe that Western countries in general, and the United States in particular, are enemies of Islam. Champions of Saudi Wahhabism blame Jews and Christians for opposing Islamic regimes, destroying their economies, corrupting young Muslims, and seducing Muslim women. Wahhabi pundits all over the world call on Muslims to wage *jihad* and join terrorist groups in order to kill Americans and other Westerners.

THE FORCES BEHIND WAHHABI IDEOLOGY

Why has Saudi Arabia, which for many years was considered by the United States as its strategic ally, become so hostile towards the West, which, after all, is the main source of Saudi wealth and prosperity? And why have Saudi business and clerical forces supported such an aggressive anti-American ideology?

FANATICAL ANTI-AMERICANISM

The end of the Cold War and the dissolution of the Soviet Union left the United States as the world's sole superpower and accelerated the growth of anti-Americanism around the world. There were many possible contributing factors; the unwillingness of some Muslim immigrants to the United States to accept the American way of life; the sometimes disrespectful behavior of American servicemen or tourists while abroad; and the eternal envy the poor and unfortunate feel toward the rich and prosperous. There is also the hatred of Islamic religious fanatics, who have become increasingly well funded as oil prices have risen. They accept neither the idea of personal freedom nor the fundamental principles upon which a free and democratic society must be based.

Growing anti-Americanism could also stem, in part, from the hostility felt toward the United States by those political forces that were on the losing side of the Cold War. It may also partly be a product of deliberate efforts intended to undermine the United States economically, morally and politically launched by some political forces and legal—and not so legal—business groups, the basic interests of which are contrary to the political and economic interests of the United States, either globally or regionally.

The broad spectrum of the causes of anti-Americanism has been the subject of intense study by analysts, journalists, and scholars.

In fact, anti-Americanism has existed since the United States first emerged as a world power in the late nineteenth and early twentieth centuries. Its reflection is found in literature and film, in the caricatures and taunts of people living outside the United States, in the refusal of French waiters to serve American tourists, and in the burning of the American flag by South Korean students.

But it is crucial to understand that only the systematic efforts of powerful, organized groups—intent upon inflicting maximum damage to the United States—permits these various forms of cultural or everyday anti-Americanism to take on more virulent and destructive forms. As we now know well, these forms include armed assaults on American embassies and warships overseas, and successful, well-planned attacks on the brain-centers and main symbols of American governmental, business and military power in the United States. It is in the destructive activity of these powerful, organized groups that we find the key to the terrorist threat that facing the United States. For purposes of analysis and clarity of thinking, we need to differentiate this threat from the more common and generally innocuous forms of antipathy toward the United States. This more destructive and virulent force, which can be called "fanatical anti-Americanism," is primarily represented by business and clerical forces that encourage the ideology of Wahhabism originating from the Sunni clergy of Saudi Arabia. A secondary strain of "fanatical anti-Americanism" has arisen within Shi'a Islam, both among Iran's ruling ayatollahs and in their extremist proxies, such as Hezbollah in Lebanon or Moqtada al-Sadr's militia in Iraq.

The framework of this project does not include an examination of Iranian and Iranian-inspired fanatical anti-Americanism. We have concentrated our attention on Wahhabi ideology in an effort to understand the deep roots of Saudi-inspired fanatical anti-Americanism, which is more prevalent and widespread.

Oil, Power and Terror

Fanatical anti-Americanism, which outlines its agenda in terms of Wahhabi ideology, is an organized political force of global terror directed at the United States and its allies. It is represented, first and foremost, by certain business and clerical groups that either control or benefit from revenues coming from the huge oil resources of Saudi Arabia. They have created and/or financed Islamic terrorist organizations who are indoctrinated in Wahhabi ideology and who implement Wahhabi ideas in their terrorist activities, in particular al-Qaeda and various terrorist groups all over the world that are inspired by Wahhabi propaganda and al-Qaeda's activities.

Until recently, the Saudi royal family and official Saudi governmental circles paid little on no attention to the dissemination of Wahhabi ideology abroad and to the efforts by certain Saudi clerical and business circles to create and support al-Qaeda and other terrorist organizations. Saudi politicians preferred to put their heads in the sand, hoping that al-Qaeda's agenda would always be anti-Western or anti-Shia, and would never threaten the very existence of the Saudi government and the interests of the Saudi royal family.

However, this neglect helped create a monster: a global network of terrorist structures that possesses enough flexibility, dynamics, human, military, financial and intellectual force to damage the political and economic system in any country in the world, including in its motherland, Saudi Arabia, and to threaten the peaceful civic community life of the entire world.

Fanatical anti-American forces that outline their agenda in terms of Wahhabi ideology are ready to ignore and overcome laws, rules, customs and traditions that regulate relations between people and countries. The fanatical anti-American network represents a new danger because it is capable of acting everywhere due to its lack of any legal political structure, by its efforts to penetrate anywhere under the cover of peaceful citizens, and by using non-traditional weapons such as exploding cars, suicide bombers, passenger planes or informational networks.

Although fanatical anti-Americanism is new on the world stage, it reminds us of German Nazism and Soviet Communism, which were known for their similar inclination to destroy "the old world," eagerness to sacrifice, readiness to ignore any rules and limits of the "evil order," Puritanism of ideas, and readiness to pay any price for them. In fanatical anti-Americanism, one easily recognizes the spirit of the revolutionary movements of the past two centuries that have traumatized the world.

Fanatical anti-Americanism has various economic and political interests in common with influential political and business circles in Russia, China, North Korea, and Cuba. It also has an array of common interests with representatives of international organized crime.

Until September 11, 2001, there were only two instances in which open military challenges were made to the United States: by German Nazism during World War II and by Soviet Communism during the Cold War. These two forces of evil aspired to world domination and the destruction of American democracy and the free market system.

Fanatical anti-Americanism, while also issuing a military challenge to the United States and its allies, has set for itself ambitious, albeit more limited goals. The forces that represent fanatical anti-Americanism are not trying to do away with the capitalist system. They understand that terror can inflict some damage on democratic freedoms and the institutions of American democracy. But terror is not capable of destroying the American state and replacing it with an Islamic caliphate. Economically, these forces seek primarily to inflict maximum damage on the U.S. economy. Their main immediate political goal is to compel the United States to terminate its military presence in the Persian Gulf region.

The "Letter to the American People," purported to have been written by Osama bin Laden or on his behalf and published in October 2002, outlined the agenda of fanatical anti-Americanism. In it, bin Laden expressed his opposition to U.S. policies in support of certain Arab and Muslim countries—which he considers "agent countries" of the United States: "The policies employed in these countries stop our nation from establishing the Islamic Shari'ah, thereby causing great harm to the *ummah*." He accused these rulers of abusing and absconding with the region's natural resources in order to enrich themselves at the expense of the destitute population: "So the removal of these policies is an individual obligation upon us so as to make the Shari'ah the supreme law and to regain Palestine. Our fight against these policies is the same as fighting against [the United States]." He lamented that it is quite difficult to overthrow the governments of these "agent countries" because of the presence of U.S. forces, whose "outrageous behavior" has further aggravated an already-complex situation: "Your forces occupy our lands spreading your ideology and thereby polluting the hearts of our people. You have laid siege on our holy places, mocking the sanctity of our mosques. You have done all of this to protect the Jews and safeguard your pillage of our treasures." [55]

The goal of fanatical anti-Americanism, presented in bin Laden's letter is to force the United States out of those countries. The forces that represent this outlook believe that the United States should "stop supporting Israel, end support of the Indians in Kashmir, the Russians against the Chechens and also cease supporting the Manila Government against the Muslims in the Southern Philippines." Most important is for all Americans "to pack your luggage and get out of our lands. We want you to have a successful and happy life, so don't force us to send you back in coffins in cargo planes." [56]

What makes fanatical anti-Americanism so arrogant and so confident in pushing its political agenda? The answer is obvious: oil and petrodollars.

By 1980, Saudi Arabia had reached full oil production. As the balance of power shifted from consumers to producers as a result of rising world demand for oil, massive numbers of petrodollars began to flow into the country. Not surprisingly, riches on this scale swelled the heads of its recipients—men whose ancestors had for centuries lived a nomadic life on the very desert sands that covered the enormous deposits of black gold. The Saudi clerical and business circles realized that the tremendous wealth flowing into their hands opened for them seemingly unlimited possibilities, not the least of which was the chance to live life on a sumptuous scale, as this term is understood in the Middle East, meaning huge palaces, luxurious automobiles, dozens and even hundreds of wives and concubines.

Money brings power, and a great deal of money brings enormous power. However, the newly rich in Saudi Arabia, upon whom money had almost literally fallen from the sky, had great difficulty understanding that real national wealth comes from the creation of industry, communications, a banking system, democratic institutions, and support for a free market economy that produces wealth. Such strengths enable a nation to create a strong army based on the industrial, scientific, and economic potential. The combination of all of these factors creates not only a nation's wealth, but also defines its economic and political potential within the world community and its global economic and political influence.

Saudi clerical and business circles, however, remained prisoners to their tribal mentality and values, despite the fact that many of them had received educations at the finest universities and military academies the West has to offer. For those with this tribal mentality, it was difficult to imagine that both money and power are the results of a developed infrastructure, science, a modern economic system and democratic institutions.

Because of the limits of their tribal consciousness, Saudi clerical and business circles came to the conclusion that can be expressed as follows:

Our money means we should have complete economic and political power in the region. It will help us end the American military presence and establish full economic and political control here. Freedom of action in our own region will give us the chance to assume political power, to buy nuclear weapons and to ensure that the United States and other powers never again interfere in our affairs.

The idea that it was possible to present a military challenge to the United States arose among Saudi clerical and business circles during the course of the Soviet war in Afghanistan. Not only the Saudi government but also powerful Saudi financial clans such as those of bin Mahfouz and bin Laden helped finance the war, recruiting and supporting Afghan and foreign fighters who conducted the guerilla war against the Soviet occupation army. At that time, Osama bin Laden used some of his father's clan's money to buy arms and hire fighters for the anti-Soviet resistance.

In 1989, the Soviet Union withdrew its forces from Afghanistan; two years later the USSR itself ceased to exist. The tribal mentality, as always, directly connected events and appearances. It refused to consider that the victory in the Afghan war would not have been possible without American military, intelligence, propaganda and political support. For those possessing this sort of consciousness it was, indeed, impossible to understand the whole complex array of economic, political and social factors that led to the dissolution of the Soviet Union. They instead embraced the following line of reasoning:

We financed this war. Our people waged it. The Americans did no more than provide us with goods and services bought with our money. Thanks to the bravery of our mujahideen, we not only routed the army of a great power, we destroyed that power itself. We are so smart that we can now challenge any superpower!

Saudi clerical and business circles understood very well that they did not have the strength to compel U.S. troops to leave through the use of conventional military force. Instead, they recognized that U.S. forces could be expelled by using terror, which in turn could be stimulated by Wahhabi ideology. Saudi clerical and business circles believe that the Wahhabi ideas that helped to establish the Saudi state in the 18th Century and to conquer neighboring Muslim emirates may help them today to topple the Saudi royal family, to take power in their own hands, to promote their own internal and external agenda, to become independent from the West and to dictate their political agenda, at least to the Muslim world.

Unlike the political leaderships of Nazi Germany and Soviet Communism, the representatives of fanatical anti-Americanism understood that they did not have the strength to drive out U.S. troops through the use of conventional military force. For that reason, the representatives of fanatical anti-Americanism chose terror as the military means and Wahhabism as the ideological tool with which they would seek to achieve their goals.

It is necessary to give the strategists of fanatical anti-Americanism their due. Possessing neither the experience, the skills, nor the desire to create a developed economic system—one capable of producing wealth—they nevertheless managed, in their sadistic way, to identify the key vulnerabilities of such a system. As a result of the September 11 terrorist attacks, carried out by nineteen Muslim fanatics, the U.S. economy suffered losses amounting to billions of dollars. And the further actions of Wahhabi terrorist organizations led to turmoil in world markets, and especially to a sharp rise of oil prices, which has brought enormous financial profits to fanatical anti-American forces and the sponsors of Wahhabism.

The strategists of fanatical anti-Americanism chose terror as the main means for battling the United States because mass terrorist activities would inevitably have a negative impact on the morale of the U.S. civilian population, which since the U.S. Civil War has not known the destruction of warfare on its own territory and which has always felt itself fully secure from the attack of any foreign power. Massive terrorist actions are intended to undermine precisely this sense of security. The representatives of fanatical anti-Americanism are hoping that the American citizenry will wilt under the threat of constant terrorist attack and under the fear of being drawn into a prolonged war in Iraq or Iran, like that which took place in Vietnam. They hope, ultimately, that the American people will demand of their lawmakers and government that the United States withdraw its troops from the Persian Gulf, end its occupation of Iraq and keep its hands off independent Islamic governments. The antiwar demonstrations that we have seen lately are evidence that the strategists of fanatical anti-Americanism are enjoying some success.

MAJOR COMPONENTS OF THE WAHHABI WORLDVIEW

Wahhabi ideological leaders use essentially Fascist and Bolshevik methods of "ideological work," in that they do not care about or represent the true essence of Islam, its culture and its values as perceived by Muslim believers or as understood by Islamic experts. All they wish to do is to find some quotations of Islamic heritage—from the Qur'an, Sunnah or hadiths—to take these quotations out

48

of context, and to use these quotations in order to justify their political or/and economic aims. Wahhabism's sponsors need these quotations to camouflage their real goals and to make these aims attractive to the Muslim public and the naïve foot-soldiers of Islamic terrorism.

For example, according to scholars Zeyno Baran, Frederick Starr & Svante Cornell, the Hizb –ut-Tahrir (HT) movement in Central Asia "effectively combines Marxist-Leninist methodology and Western-style slogans with reactionary Islamist ideology to shape the internal debate within Islam. As an organization, HT also bears striking similarities to the early Bolshevik movement. Both have an ultimate, utopian political goal (whether "true communism" or the Caliphate), and both show an intense dislike for liberal democracy, while seeking to establish a mythical "just society." Both also function with a secretive cell system. And… HT does justify the use of force, just as Lenin and the Bolsheviks did in 1917."[57]

There are strong reasons to believe that champions of Wahhabism know very well and/or have intuited the methods of propaganda or "ideological work" that were once taught at Soviet party schools to members of Islamic governments in Third World countries and Muslim leaders of national liberation movements. According to Soviet methods, ideology is not the same as theory. Rather it translates the interest of the political leaders into theoretical terms with mass appeal to the target audience. For example, the communist ideology developed by the Communist Party of the Soviet Union was not the same as Marxist theory. Rather, the Bolsheviks adapted some ideas from Marxist theory as suitable "clothing" for the pursuit of their goal to maximize their own power. And the Bolsheviks were careful to propagate only certain Marxist ideas and terms—those which fit their self-interest—rather than the entirety of Marxism thought.

For instance, before 1956, Marx's and Engel's book *The German Ideology,* was virtually prohibited in the USSR because its content contradicted official communist ideology. The book forecast that a society that made the state the sole owner of property would be much worse than a capitalist society because monopolist state property is the worst type of property—"the marasmus [agony] of mutual private property." Bolshevik ideologists could not countenance a book that referred to their society in this fashion.

The Wahhabis ideologists take exactly the same dishonest, exploitative, selective approach to Islamic theology and its major sources, the Qur'an and Sunnah, as communist ideologists did towards Marx's thought. Since Islamic theology is a rather eclectic collection of contradictory ideas, extremists and fanatics have exploited its potential for misinterpretation, in order to further their own goals, for centuries.

When the Bolsheviks converted Marxist ideology into one of the main tools of their apparatus of power, they had to eliminate all opposition to this ideology. Such opposition might come from champions of social theories that confronted and contradicted the Bolshevik or "communist" ideology. In order to eradicate this possible theoretical competition, the Bolsheviks decided to eliminate philosophers and other social science scholars who understood that communist ideology had little to do with Marxist theory. In August 1922, Lenin blessed the forced deportation of prominent Russian philosophers, sociologists and economists. Among those deported were such famous scholars as Nikolai Berdyaev, Nikolai Lossky, Semen Frank, Vasiliy Zenkovski, Lev Karsavin, Ivan Il'in, Ivan Lapshin, Lev Shestov, Fyodor Stepun, and Boris Vysheslavtsev. Ironically, the social scientists and scholars who were deported from Russia in 1922 were lucky; six years later they would have gone to the labor camps of the GULAG, where Stalin and his successors sent their theoretical opponents.

Soviet researcher Dr. Yuri Afanasiev characterized the communist attitude towards ideological debate as, "we are ready for consensus with anybody provided that our faith is acknowledged as the only true one."[58] Champions of Wahhabism demonstrate the same intolerance towards the long-established, major Muslim schools of thought and Islamic experts who do not accept their vision of Islam and Islamic theology. Wahhabism seeks to convince Muslims that the traditional Islamic principles of belief have been lost by other Muslim schools of thought and contemporary Islamic experts, especially those who represent tolerant *mazhabs* (schools of Islamic theology) of Islam. For example, the founder of Wahhabism—Ibn Abd al-Wahhab—did not recognize the traditional *mazhabs* and arbitrarily commented upon the *ayahs* (verses) of the Holy Qur'an and hadiths of the Prophet Muhammad, relying only on his personal understanding and rejecting the opinions of other *alims* (Islamic experts) and the Muslim ummah (community). The *fatwa* "Is it possible to call Muhammad ibn Abd al-Wahhab an *alim*?," which was disseminated by the Religious Department of Muslims in Dagestan and other republics of the North Caucasus, states:

> *Alim*s are those people who are knowledgeable about the Muslim religion and strictly follow all the prescriptions of Allah. The *alim*s accept the Holy Qur'an, hadiths and all four *mazhabs*... Muhammad ibn Abd al-Wahhab criticized *"ashabs"*—the Companions of the Prophet... and distorted their views. He rejected the hadiths in which the *ashabs* were given an honorable place. He looked down on the admonition of the Prophet Muhammad (PBUH) who taught us, "Follow my *ashabs*; they will guide you to the true path."

> A most profound delusion of Muhammad ibn Abd al-Wahhab was that he labeled as *kafirs* [disbelievers] all those who refused to follow his ideology. In doing this, he rejected the admonition of the Prophet (PBUH): "Whoever calls a Muslim *kafir*, he expresses by himself his disbelief toward Allah." It is absolutely obvious that Muhammad ibn Abd al-Wahhab was not an *alim*; a true *alim* aims to help a man find the right path, while Muhammad ibn Abd al-Wahhab deluded his followers. His teachings, which contradict the Holy Qur'an and the hadiths, became the basis for dangerous tendencies in the ummah, and caused enmity and animosity among Muslims."[59]

Hatred of Christians, Jews, and Other "Infidels"

Wahhabis condemn all non-Muslims as "infidels." The founder of Wahhabism, Muhammad ibn Abd al-Wahhab, wrote that only Muslims can be considered righteous believers: "Nobody except a Muslim is considered a believer and righteous, even the apostles and messengers of Allah who came before Muhammad (PBUH)."[60] In his classic text, *The Book of Monotheism*, ibn Abd al-Wahhab characterized Jews and Christians as polytheists: "If a believer belongs to the People of the Book [Jews and Christians], he is a polytheist (mushrik), as he does not understand the real essence of monotheism."[61] Imam ibn Udoma al-Maksidi stated: "A man educated not by Islam and the Sunnah is a heretic."[62]

Wahhabis often group together Christians and Jews for attack. Muhammad Qutb, the brother of former Muslim Brotherhood leader Sayyid Qutb, taught in Saudi Arabia at King Abdul Aziz University, where one of his students was Osama bin Laden. This is how Qutb describes Jews and Christians: "The Jews displayed disbelief toward Jesus and Muhammad. The Christians rejected Muhammad and believed in Jesus, but not as an apostle. They believed that Jesus is God and the Son of God."[63] "The Jews hate Christians. They display enmity towards Muslims as well. In the same way, Christians do not like Muslims because of Muhammad (PBUH) and the Qur'an."[64]

Ibn Taymiya, an Islamic scholar of the 13th and 14th Century favored by Wahhabis, considered both Jews and Christians to be "polytheists," characterizing Jews as "cursed" and "arrogant" and Christians as "deluded."[65] The founder of Wahhabism, Muhammad ibn abd al-Wahhab, considered Jews and Christians to be mortal enemies of Islam: "Hypocritical Jews and Christians do not like the commandments of Allah and the Prophet Muhammad (PBUH). Hypocrites are avid enemies of believers. Both in the past and today… we can see this in their enmity against Muslims and efforts to eliminate the ray of Islam and belief."[66]

Wahhabis consider Jews and Christians to be misguided unbelievers because they rejected Muhammad. For example, the former Saudi Grand Mufti Abd al-Aziz bin Baz characterized Jews and Christians as "deluded unbelievers" because "even if Jews and Christians are monotheists, they are still deluded unbelievers because they do not believe in Muhammad (PBUH)."[67] Muhammad ibn Dzhamil Zinu defines those who do not follow Islam as "preachers of evil:" "The preachers of evil are those who are not guided by the life of the Allah's Messenger (PBUH) in their lives, program and their authority. These people do not follow the Prophet (PBUH) in their appearance, clothes, customs and traditions. Every Muslim should beware of them."[68]

Wahhabis consider Christianity's doctrine of the Trinity to be the ultimate expression of blasphemy because it deifies Jesus and, in their opinion, ascribes other partners to the one, true God. Ibn Abd al-Wahhab thus condemns Christians and others as polytheists, stating that it is acceptable to kill them: "Their [Christians'] references to angels and prophets and asking for their intercession to get closer to Allah is what makes it acceptable to spill their blood [kill them] and take their property."[69] Ibn Taymiya categorizes Christians as "unbelievers" because they believe that "Allah is in Jesus while Jesus exists in the body of a man."[70]

Wahhabis endorse the idea that Muslims and Islam are superior to Christians and Jews and their religions. Abdul Rahman Ben Hammad Al-Omar states that those who do not believe in Islam cannot be faithful followers of Jesus, Moses, or the prophets of other religions:

> No one should adopt any religion other than Islam, the perfect and true religion, which supercedes all other religions. As for Judaism and Christianity, they have both been changed and perverted. On the other hand, every Muslim following Muhammad is, at the same time, a follower of Moses, Jesus, and the other prophets. Every unbeliever in Islam is also an unbeliever in Moses, Jesus and other prophets, even if he pretends to be one of their followers. This explains why many Jewish rabbis and Christian monks hastened to embrace Islam and believe in Muhammad.[71]

According to Ibn Taymiya, Muslims know more than the followers of other faiths:

> Does the Muslim *ummah* (community) know less than small-minded people who are lower than they are, in particular, in learning about Allah, understanding his commandments and deep knowledge of the miracles of Allah? How can demagogues—philosophers, followers of Indian and Greek philosophy, fire-worshippers, those who ascribe partners to Allah, Jews, Christians, Sabeans (those who worship stars) and the like—know more than Muslims?![72]

Ibn Taymiya says Christians are inferior to Muslims because they place Jesus and other humans on equal terms with God, and Jews are inferior because they killed the prophets who tried to bring them the word of God.[73] Taqi al-Din Nabhanii states that Islam is superior to Judaism because it is a universal religion, for all nationalities, and that it is superior to Christianity because Christianity is only concerned with the afterlife, not life on earth.[74]

Wahhabis encourage Muslims to actively hate Christians and Jews. Muhammad ibn Abd al-Wahhab teaches Muslims to "maintain hatred against" non-Muslims.[75] Muhammad Qutb says that Jews and Christians oppress and kill Muslims: "Muslims living under the rule of Jews and Christians suffer a great deal. Their property and land are expropriated and they are humiliated and insulted. Jews and Christians kill hundreds of thousands of Muslims."[76]

Wahhabis encourage every Muslim to develop enmity between himself and unbelievers: "An expression of contempt and hostility toward the most malicious and the unbelievers is a witness of perfect belief."[77] Authors of a book about Muhammad ibn Abd al-Wahhab say that Muslims should "break all relations" with "unbelievers" and hate them: "Even if an unbeliever is your brother; he is your enemy in religion. It is a sin for any Muslim to maintain a friendship with an unbeliever…Muslims must treat them as enemies, keep hatred in their hearts against them and be at enmity with them… Allah blesses those Muslims who kindle hatred in themselves against [unbelievers]."[78] Dr. Yusus Ardaui defines "unbelievers" as enemies of Muslims, even if they are relatives of a Muslim:

> Islam does not condone friendly relations with people of other convictions and divides people according to whether they are believers or unbelievers. If this is so, a *kafir* [unbeliever] enemy is an enemy of Islam and an enemy of Muslims, even though he may be a neighbor of Muslims in one country and one of representatives of his nation; even if he is a brother of his father or mother.[79]

Wahhabis condemn any peaceful coexistence between Muslims and non-Muslims: "There is nothing except iron between unbelievers and Muslims."[80] Moreover, they believe that apostates should be put to death. Muhammad ibn Abd al-Wahhab stated that blasphemers can be killed and their property appropriated: "Belief in what is prohibited by Allah and the Prophet (PBUH) shall be considered as blasphemy. This opens up a path to his soul and property [that is, such a person can be murdered and his property can be appropriated]."[81] Former Saudi Grand Mufti Bin Baz states that opponents of Islam should be killed or jailed: "Whoever is secretly or openly against the way of Muhammad (PBUH), he has disbelief or hypocrisy in his heart. His punishment in this world should be death or imprisonment."[82] Muhammad ibn Salih al'-'Useimin says Jews and Christians should be killed: "We are convinced that everyone who considers Jewish, Christian or any other beliefs to be correct and comprehensible in the face of Allah is unfaithful and an atheist. If he or she repents of this, Allah will forgive them. If not, they deserve death as an apostate who denies the Qur'an."[83]

Wahhabi hatred for Jews has a long history. Abid Tawfiq al-Hashimi associates Jews with "world evil."[84] Muti' an-Nuvnav claims that Jews wish to destroy civilization: "All the disasters in the world are result of putting into practice the 'shining' morals of the Jews in the Talmud. The Jews have wanted to destroy the basis of civilization for many centuries. They are still trying to accomplish this."[85]

Wahhabis always claim that Jews fall under God's curse: "...they are not accepted by God; how could the Almighty entrust to them testaments about owning the Holy Land?! According to the conviction of the Torah, they were exiled because they were born from a sinful generation!"[86]

Muhammad Qutb claims that Jews are uniquely evil: "Allah cursed them from generation to generation. Jews have committed more evil than any other nation has."[87] The Wahhabis condemn Jewish beliefs and religion. Muhammad ibn Dzhamil Zinu associates Judaism with "every destructive doctrine."[88] Wahhabis usually describe Zionism in terms of conspiracy. Abid Tawfiq al-Hashimi claims:

> ...the idea 'Zion is Mecca' appears among the People of the Book! And this was hidden from the world public! If it was hidden, it means Jewish Zionist goals aim for far more than Palestine and Jerusalem! Mecca is also their goal! Those who read the Zionist protocols and Jewish Zionist decisions understand that they aim at enslaving humanity; if one analyzes Zionist policy, he will discover Jewish plans, which try to make Islam distant from people, change its essence, keep Islam out of life, thoughts and laws, spread sexual and moral debauchery, mix women and men in private and public places; they attempt to depict Islam as defined by Jewish spies as an extremist, obsolete, segregated and dogmatic religion; thus they create a hostile environment toward Islam; these are all intended to deny people enthusiasm about Islam, deny their hearts love for Islam, deny their thoughts respect for the religion—which, as an end result, means the beginning of opening the way to Zion-Mecca!!![89]

Muti' an-Nuvnav also claims that Jews wish to destroy Islam:

> The Islamic world, in particular the Arab world, faces enemies that are not tired or compassionate, but determined to destroy the Islamic Shari'ah. World Masonry and the Protocols of Zionists are aimed at alienating Islamic nations from their convictions, religion and Shari'ah. They are aimed at liquidating the roots of the Islamic religion...[90]

Hatred against Muslims who do not agree with the Wahhabi Interpretation of Islam

Wahhabi authorities condemn as "apostates" those Muslims who dare to show toleration for infidels. Muhammad ibn Dzhamil Zinu believes that true Muslims have to "behave with hostility toward polytheists and unbelievers."[91] "Every true Muslim must necessarily show enmity and feel hatred toward pagans and display this openly. Hatred concealed in the heart is useless, until it is openly revealed as enmity and boycott. When friendship and strong relations take place, this is evidence of the absence of hatred."[92]

Wahhabis claim that Sufi, Shi'ite and other non-Wahhabi interpretations of Islam are not true Islam. Muhammad ibn Dzhamil Zinu says that "Sufism did not exist in the era of the Messenger of Allah (PBUH), his companions and Taba'een [i.e., the "followers"—the several generations of people who lived in the period of the Companions of the Prophet (PBUH), after the Prophet (PBUH), and who did not see the Prophet (PBUH)]. It arose later, when some Greek books were translated into the Arabic language... In many questions, Sufism disagrees with Islam."[93] Wahhabis hate Shi'as and label Shi'a Islam as a Jewish or English invention against Islam. Abdul Rahman ben Hammad Al-Omar castigates as unbelievers both Shi'ite Muslims and smaller sects who consider themselves to be Muslims. His hatred directed mostly against Shi'ites:

> Among the sects that deviated from the straight path of Islam, although they claim to be Muslims, is the large sect of the Shi'a. The followers of this sect pretend to be Muslims, i.e., they pray, fast and perform the Hajj... [However,] Muslims throughout the world should know that these sects and all other enemies of Islam cooperate and strive hard to destroy Islam.[94]

Modern Wahhabis strictly follow the legacy of Ibn Abd al-Wahhab. A famous imam from the city of Andijon in Uzbekistan, Abduvali kori Mirzoev, stated in a sermon that Imam Ahmad ibn Hanbal (the founder of the Hanbali school of thought, which is close to Wahhabism) appealed to his followers to not recognize the founders of the other *mazhabs* (schools of thought)—Abu Hanifa, Imam Malik and Imam ash-Shafi'i.[95] The author of the booklet *The Religion of Truth is Islam* also states that, "a Muslim is not obliged to follow one of the schools of thought in Islam."[96]

Wahhabis force other Muslims to follow their codes of behavior. An audiotape distributed among Central Asian pilgrims who visited Saudi Arabia for the Hajj in 2004 laid out very strict requirements for being considered a true Muslim:

> There is a minimum standard to which every Muslim should adhere. A Muslim is not considered to be a Muslim if he does not meet this minimum. The minimum requirement... is observance of the Shari'ah of Allah, not turning away from it. The one who turns away from it and lives by other norms, not the Shari'ah of Allah—this person fails to fulfill the minimum; he does not pass this exam, and therefore he has left Islam... even if he makes *namaz* (prayer), keeps the fast, gives *zakat*, does the Hajj and states that he is a Muslim.

The audiotape also condemned allegiance to one's country or other doctrines as equivalent to worshipping "false deities."

Abdul Rahman ben Hammad Al-Omar believes that those Muslims who disagree with Wahhabis "contradict Islam."[97] Muhammad ibn Abd al-Wahhab insists that those who do not accept and follow the dictates of Islam completely are disbelievers, who can be killed and have their property taken.[98] Muhammad Qutb claims that Muslims who "imitate" others in their laws and customs can not be "true Muslims."[99]

Dr. Sayyid Abul A'la Mawdudi describes the conditions that must exist, from the Wahhabi's point of view, for a person who wants to be a "true Muslim." He states that

> to be born in a Muslim house, to bear a Muslim name, to dress as a Muslim and to call oneself a Muslim is insufficient in order to become a Muslim... The real difference between a *kafir* (a person who does not accept Divine guidance and shows ingratitude to Him) and a Muslim lies not in the name; let it be Smith, Ram, Lal or Abdullah. The name does not determine who is the *kafir* and who is the Muslim. Tie and turban are also not reasons to differentiate between them. The difference lies in knowledge. A *kafir* does not understand his connection with God. Since he does not know the Divine will, he cannot know the correct course of life.[100]... If Muslims are as ignorant about the Islam as *kafirs* are, why should one consider them as being above *kafirs*, and why should they have a different destiny?"[101]

Mawdudi makes particular efforts to define the difference between "true Muslims," i.e. Wahhabis, and non-Wahhabi Muslims:

> Non-Muslims are those people who, instead of following the Qur'an and Sunnah, submit to the dictatorship of their own desires, adhere to the customs of their ancestors, accept everything that occurs in society, and never bother to consult the Qur'an and Sunnah to learn how to handle their business, or refuse to accept the doctrine of the Qur'an and Sunnah at all, saying 'They do not suit me' or 'They are against the customs of my ancestors,' or 'The world moves in the opposite direction.' Such people lie when they call themselves Muslims.... It is contradictory to call oneself a Muslim and at the same time to follow one's own opinions, society's customs, or any person's words, if they are against the Qur'an and Sunnah."[102]... You call yourselves Muslims and yet serve *kufr* [disbelief] devotedly, receive interest, insure your live, and deceive in court; your daughters and wives have forgotten Islamic manners and your children have obtained a secular education. Some people followed the apostles of Gandhi; others followed Lenin."[103]

Hatred against Western Democracy, Culture and Way of Life

The basic Islamic texts do not specify any uniquely Islamic form of political system, such as a caliphate, kingdom, or an Islamic republic. However, the Wahhabis have sought to prevent Western democratic ideas from spreading and try to present democracy as something that threatens Islam and contradicts Islamic values.

The Wahhabis talk about the impending collapse of Western democracy because, according to their doctrine, one should not follow a secular ideology or obey secular laws because all secular ideologies and civic laws were created by man, not by God. According to the Wahhabis, any sociopolitical system that is not based entirely, completely and solely on the Shari'ah, as the Wahhabis understand it, is a form of "unbelief." Unbelief is characterized as "a rule and a judgment that has a basis that was not granted by Allah."[104] Any human legislative or norms-producing activity is declared to be "unbelief." Unbelief is defined as "the claim to have the right to issue laws, permissions and restrictions."[105] Wahhabis label as "unbelievers" everyone who participates in the public welfare system, which delegates power and redistributes public resources, as well as the exchange of services.

Muhammad Qutb condemns Western economic and political systems, because:

> capitalism is a spoiled and ignorant system. It is constructed on mercenary relations that are forbidden by Allah. [In capitalist society,] a small group of people spend their wealth on moral debauchery in order to crush human dignity. Laws are also issued by this unfair class. They do not apply the Shari'ah [Law] of Allah. This means that capitalism is a spiteful, ignorant deviation from the true path.[106]

Muti' an-Nuvnav portrays Western systems as "cynical" and "sinful."[107] Taqi al-Din Nabhanii condemns Western democracy because "in Western countries the capitalist system rules the governments and makes their activities dependent on capitalists to such a degree that the capitalists are the real rulers in the countries that have embraced the capitalist ideology..."[108]

Wahhabis reject the Western political system, which separates religion and politics. Wahhabis predict that capitalism will collapse "because capitalist ideology separates religion from life, drives religion out of social relations and considers it merely as a matter of one's personal conscience. This hinders Allah's system, which is to participate in worldly affairs and to have a beneficial effect on them."[109] Taqi al-Din Nabhanii believes:

> The principle of the separation of religion from worldly affairs and the exclusion of religion from any impact on public affairs is the foundation of Western culture. The separation of religion from the state is a natural consequence of the principle according to which religion is separate from anything material. ... The main goal of life is material profit. Human actions are evaluated according to the criteria of whether they contribute to making a profit. Profit is the sole criterion used for building the entire system and creating its culture. This criterion is a basis for all social and cultural concepts, which describe the goal of life as the acquisition of wealth.[110]

Muhammad Qutb criticizes what he sees as the harmful effects of separating religion from public life: "Europe has eliminated religion from real life, enclosing it in the narrow framework limited by one's individual conscience. But people can not maintain a healthy conscience if they have separated themselves from religion!"[111]

Wahhabis teach that Western culture is unacceptable for Muslims: "Islam is against moral lechery and the social, political and economic humiliations of the capitalist West!"[112] An audiotape distributed among Central Asian pilgrims who visited Saudi Arabia for the Hajj in 2004 criticized Western materialism:

> In the modern world, or in the modern *jahiliyya* [ignorance] existing in the West… there are some objects of worship. For instance, the dollar. What place does it occupy in the heart of its owner? It is a worshipped deity. Although no temples are built to it and no prayers are made to it, it still holds sway over people… so, it is the object of worship. The Messenger of Allah (PBUH) was right when he said, 'The slave of the dinar [Arab gold coin] is miserable, and the slave of dirham [Arab silver coin] is miserable.' And now we can say that the slave of the dollar is miserable too."

The Russian translation of Dr. Sayyid Abul A'la Mawdudi' book *Let us be Muslims* paints a dark picture of Western society for Central Asian readers:

> Your opinion that the believers in *kalima* kabita ["the false word," a for Western society] prosper in this world is fallacious. In a true sense, these people have never succeeded and do not succeed now. You look at their excessive wealth, their magnificent luxury and externally deceptive magnificence. But material prosperity is not true. Let their souls reveal how many of them have reached peace. They wallow in luxury, but their hearts are… nervous and disconsolate. What Hell have their houses been turned into because of their disobedience to the laws of God? How many suicides are there in Europe and America? How common is divorce? How many people have they destroyed through genocide, birth control and abortions? How many thousands of lives have been destroyed by drugs and alcohol? How furious is the struggle for markets and economic well-being among nations and classes? How have envy, jealousy and hatred set people against each other? How has this mad battle for more material benefits made life bitter for so many people? And what about the modern huge, magnificent cities, which look like paradise from afar, but which contain thousands

and thousands of people vegetating in poverty? Can you call this prosperity? Do you really wish for this so enviously?[113]

Taqi al-Din Nabhanii compares Islamic and European cultures and concludes that Western life is nothing but a soulless search for material wealth and profit,[114] and that Western culture is a disaster for the human race.[115] And Muhammad Qutb predicts that Western civilization will collapse, just as the Soviet Union fell:

> We remind people who consider the crash of Western civilization to be impossible of the destruction of the greatest force of oppression in history, namely, the force of communism as represented by the former Soviet Union, which literally broke up in front of our eyes. Now it is the turn of the West...[116]

Wahhabis condemn Muslim governments that do not rule by rigid, Wahhabi-style Shari'ah. Wahhabis label existing Muslim governments as secular because they follow mostly Western-style laws and a Western-style legal code. They consider almost all the present ruling regimes in Muslim countries as "barbarian" or "pseudo-Islamic." These leaders are accused of apostasy, bribery and corruption; of unacceptably close relations to the West, in particular, the United States, the dissemination and transplantation of Western culture and, consequently, the destruction of decency and moral decay.

The goal of Wahhabis is to establish an Islamic caliphate. In view of the fact that, according to Wahhabi doctrine, the majority of existing regimes in Arab and Muslim countries are illegal, the Wahhabis believe that they have all "legitimate justifications" to overthrow them. Non-Muslim countries must also be the subject of violent Islamization.

Taqi al-Din Nabhanii claims that all Muslim states are actually anti-Islamic: "The state of Islam was destroyed and the dream of the West about the destruction of the Islamic state came true. After the destruction of the Islamic state, all the governments of Islamic states became against Islam. Muslims began living under the flag against Islam."[117] Muhammad Qutb blames all government that do not rule by Islamic Shari'ah.[118] He criticizes the Western public's participation in creating laws: "When democracy grants the right of legislation (that is, the right to mandate sanctions and prohibitions) to people instead of the Allah, it becomes… the sin of polytheism and consequently can be characterized as ignorance, from the point of view of Divine criteria."[119] Muhammad Qutb tries to evaluate democracy according to the norms of Islam and discovers its two faces: "a rather light face of democracy, which gives a person rights and guarantees against the arbitrariness of the state, and the other face, black as resin, which permits atheism under the pretext of allowing freedom of worship, as well as sexual and moral dissoluteness under the pretext of allowing personal freedom."[120] According to Muhammad Qutb, if Muslims obey governments, the rule of which depends on force and lacks Allah's support, this shows that "Muslims became weak to the point where the successors of the Crusaders and the Zionists dominate them. If they allow this and agree with it, they will be punished in the flames of Hell!"[121]

Materials disseminated by Hizb ut-Tahrir claim that "[i]t is indisputable that an Islamic state will emerge, being strong, sustainable and capable of war. Its *Aqidah* [worldview] is a doctrine for all humankind, and therefore it is a global system of life. Because of this, naturally, the Islamic state will conquer other countries. The system of Islam obliges it to invade other countries."[122] According to the Wahhabi plan, a revived caliphate would include northern Africa, the Arabian peninsula, the countries of the Near and Middle East, the western part of India, Central Asia, and the northern Caucasus.

For Wahhabis, human rights are another weapon used by infidels to attack and undermine Islam. Muhammad Qutb states:

> Western democracy claims that it invented human rights. This statement is false… Europe 'observes' them only in books, in state constitutions, and in some pieces of legislation… However, this 'freedom' sows discord. On the one hand, it eases the way to heresy and to faithlessness, and to various kinds of moral debauchery. And, on the other hand, such 'freedom' puts rigid obstacles in place as soon as capitalist interests are endangered. In both instances, such 'freedom' does not benefit people![123]

Wahhabi intolerance towards human rights exposes itself most clearly in the suppression of women. The Wahhabis do not consider women to be equal to men either in a material or legal sense and do not conceal this attitude. The

Wahhabis do not allow women to participate in public life, downgrade them to the position of illiterates, and restrict them to running the household and raising children. The clearest example of the Wahhabi attitude toward women was displayed in Afghanistan, where the Taliban demonstrated to the whole world how Wahhabis treat women.

Wahhabis consider women to be a cause of sinful behavior, which, if allowed, would undermine social and moral norms and rules. Wahhabis believe that women must be segregated from men behind closed doors, or beneath veils and chadors. Wahbiy Suleyman Gaudji al-Albani sets out many stringent rules for women's conduct:

> A woman should not go out to the bazaar and the society of men. Women should not mix with men in bazaars, on public transportation, or in shops. Even if relatives and friends of the husband accompany her, it is forbidden to mix with them because they may wish an evil to a woman. Perhaps such mingling will bring a sin to a woman. It is forbidden to go to the puppet theatre, listen to licentious melodies or songs... A television set should not be placed in the woman's room as television mostly causes debauchery. A woman wants what a man wants but very often instead of permitted things she wants the forbidden ones.[124]

In her book *Make your Dignity Happy*, Maysar bint Yasin says that "mingling of men and women" in public is forbidden,[125] and "inviting a woman to the place where men work" is "a great danger."[126]

Dr. Ardaui stresses the importance of strict female modesty, so as not to tempt men:

> Women are prohibited to go out of the home and attract the attention of men.[127]... The best thing is when a Muslim woman seriously wants to hide her jewels and charms. If she can, she has to hide her face. The reason is this: otherwise, there would be a great increase in debauchery and sinful deeds. If a woman is beautiful, it is important that she does not seduce a man away from the right path. A woman has to hide herself in an obligatory manner.[128]

An audiotape distributed among Central Asian pilgrims who visited Saudi Arabia for the Hajj in 2004 criticizes those who dress fashionably:

> You see a girl walking on the street, showing off her body, breaking the rules of Shari'ah. And when you ask her why she violates it, she answers that 'It is fashionable and I cannot contradict fashion.' Allah orders her not to parade her body. However, she submits to the deity 'Fashion' and cannot disobey it.[129]

According to Wahhabi thinking, women should stay at home and remain in traditional roles. Maysar bint Yasin presents this idea very clearly. She believes that if a Muslim woman has a father, brother or husband, she does not need to work outside her home.[130] Yasin is very unhappy "over the fact that the number of working women is increasing and most of them put their profession above family household duties and the education of their sons... If a mother in the house of her husband fulfills her obligations, she will never be a burden. Sewing or knitting does not contradict the feminine nature."[131]

Wahhabis are convinced that women must be controlled at all times in order to prevent them from committing sins. In *Fatwas of the Modern World*, Dr. Yusus Ardaui warns women against the temptations of the modern world: "Today, the temptations for women are stronger than never before. Destroyers use women as a weapon to ruin moral values in the name of progress and development... A Muslim woman must feel and foresee these temptations and must not become a weapon in the hands of the enemies of Islam."[132] In an earlier edition of the same book, Dr. Ardaui underlines that strict norms are necessary because men and especially women are prone to temptation: "It is forbidden for a man to look at a woman. The reason for the prohibition is the threat of temptation. A woman is more inclined to temptation, as she is more temperamental and often does not act using the intellect. Therefore, temptation affects women much more."[133] In his other book *Permitted and Forbidden Things in Islam*, Dr. Ardaui says those who want women to have the freedom to engage in ordinary jobs outside the home aim to cheapen and exploit women.[134]

Wahhabis blame Western culture as the main force corrupting Muslim women. Maysar bint Yasin warns against European freedoms for women, which, she says, are aimed at exploiting them.[135]

Solih ben 'Avzan ben Abdallah al-'Avzan warns that "unbelievers" wish to corrupt Muslim women in order to destroy Islam: "A Muslim woman in Islam achieved respect, moral purity and defense. But enemies of Islam or, more correctly, enemies of all humankind—*kafirs* [unbelievers] and hypocrites—envy the position of Muslim women. These enemies of Islam—*kafirs* and hypocrites—want to use women as a weapon to liquidate Islam."[136]

Interpretation of Holy War [Jihad]

Armed *jihad* is a core idea of Wahhabi doctrine.[137] Wahhabism asserts that *jihad* should be waged against all "unbelievers," "followers of polytheism" and "hypocrites." The Wahhabis specify several different types of *jihad*. For example, the Wahhabi scholar Muhammad ibn Dzhamil Zinu, in his book *Islamic Aqidah according to the Holy Qur'an and Authentic Sunnah*,[138] defines four types of *jihad*:

1. *jihad* against shaitan (devil)
2. *jihad* against soul
3. *jihad* against unbelievers
4. *jihad* against hypocrites.

In the materials Wahhabis have distributed in Central Asia, they do not reveal details about the meanings of "*jihad* against shaitan" or "*jihad* against soul." All Wahhabi postulates on *jihad* basically dwell on *jihad* against those whom the Wahhabis label as "unbelievers," "followers of polytheism" and "hypocrites." *Jihad* is considered to be "an armed struggle based on Islamic fundamentals," "defending the interests of Allah through arms."[139] If *jihad*—In the Wahhabi interpretation—is mostly an armed struggle, then it is clear why Wahhabi texts do not contain deliberations on "*jihad* against soul" (i.e., regarding moral self-improvement).

Wahhabis teach that all Muslims must wage *jihad* against unbelievers. Muti' an-Nuvnav says *jihad* is "one of the values of which Muslims are proud."[140] Muhammad Qutb exalts *jihad* as the most worthy activity: "The servant of God, truly believing in Allah, certainly will conduct a holy war [*jihad*] in order to realize the truth."[141] Hanafi Abdullah al-Hanafi and Muhammad Muharram al-Misri want Muslims to believe that those who wage *jihad* will ascend to the highest levels of heaven: "*Jihad* is the best work for Allah. Those who make *jihad* for the cause of Allah, He will raise to the highest levels of paradise and forgive all their sins.[142] In an earlier edition of their same book, they enumerate the rewards for those who are martyred during *jihad*: "If those people who commit *jihad* for the cause of Allah become shahids [martyrs], Allah raises them to paradise or returns them to their homeland safe and sound, with the property of their enemies."[143]

The Wahhabis see *jihad* as an important part of a long Islamic tradition. Abderrahman al'-Hanbalii an-Nadzhdii glorifies *jihad* as the "pinnacle" of Islam: "*Jihad* is a greatest and best way to work for the good. *Jihad* is the pinnacle of Islam."[144] Abdurrahman Ben Nasyr as-Saadij reiterates this thought: "*Jihad* on the way of Allah is the pinnacle of the religion."[145]

Wahhabis believe the early wars that spread Islam are a model for mandatory *jihad* or holy war. Al'-Hanbalii an-Nadzhdii describes how the founder of Wahhabism expanded the scope of *jihad*:

> Shaykh ul-Islam Muhammad ibn Abd al-Wahhab says: '*Jihad* was indicated in several stages: Initially, only permission for *jihad* was declared but then it became obligatory. Then, it was commanded not to fight with people who co-existed with Muslims in peace. It was forbidden to fight with people with whom a truce had been signed. Then, Allah commanded Muslims to break these truces and fight with all polytheists. If People of the Book [Jews and Christians] do not accept Islam, it is also obligatory to fight [them]... Even if they live peacefully with Muslims and even if they sign a truce, war against them must not be stopped.'[146] Ibn al-Kayum summarizes this vision of *jihad* becoming progressively broader: 'Initially *jihad* was forbidden, then it was permitted, then it was commanded to fight against those who first declared war, then it was commanded to fight against all polytheists.'[147]

In his book *Unforgivable Sins*, Muhammad ibn Abd al-Wahhab says *jihad* will continue until evil is extinguished: "*Jihad* will continue from the day Allah sent Muhammad (PBUH) until the last member of the ummah [community of Muslims] fights with ad-Dajjal [the Antichrist]. No crimes by tyrants nor the righteous affairs of the just can stop this [*jihad*]."[148] Abdul Rahman ben Hammad al-Omar urges conducting *jihad* until everyone converts to Islam: "If they [unbelievers] reject Islam, and do not obey Allah, Muslims must commit *jihad* against unbelievers in order to avoid conspiracy and make all the religions the religion of Allah."[149]

Wahhabism has consistently been used for military-political purposes, such as the religious justification of military campaigns and the use of violence against Muslim neighbors of the Saudi dynasty. As early as 1746, only two years after Wahhabism became the official religion of the Saudi dynasty, the new Saudi state declared *jihad* against all neighboring Muslim tribes that refused to follow this doctrine. Until the 1920s, the history of the Saudi dynasty was a history of violent acts with the purpose of forcing other Muslims to accept political and theological obedience.

Dr.Yusus Ardaui says Muslims should wage *jihad* in order to return to power in states that were once ruled by Muslims:

> *Jihad* is a movement of liberation of Islamic land from occupants—
> *kafirs* as well as changing local governors—by the commandment of
> Allah. These *kafirs* are Jews, Christians or atheists, for disbelievers have
> one nationality... If capitalists from the West, communists from the
> East, or atheists invade even one part of Islamic land, it is necessary
> to fight against them... Muslims have never been under the rule of
> *kafirs* in any Century, until now. For example, Palestine is now under
> rule of adventurers—Jews. Also, Kashmir is now under the rule of
> polytheists—Hindus. Former Islamic lands—Bukhara, Samarkand,
> Tashkent—are in the hands of unfair atheist-communists... The
> return of all these lands to Islam and liberating them from *kafirs* is
> a holy act for all Muslims. A declaration of war for the liberation of
> these lands is an Islamic obligation... If a war takes place in order to
> liberate land from unfaithful governors and the unfairness of *kafirs*,
> this war is doubtlessly a *jihad* on the way of Allah.[150]

According to Mawdudi, a Muslim's "sacred duty" is to take part in *jihad* in order to seize power in a country to ensure that the government is guided by God's will:

> Just to believe in God and His laws is not enough. As soon as you
> have believed in these two things, the sacred duty is incumbent on
> you: wherever you are, whatever country you live in, you should aspire

to correct the mistakes of the government and to take power in your hands, and away from those who are not afraid of God. You should also ensure the rule over the Divine servants and that the government conducts its business according to God's laws, so that they always realize the presence of the Lord and their accountability before Him in the future life. The name of this aspiration is *jihad*.[151]

Wahhabis encourage an "us-versus-them" mentality, in order to foster hostility among Muslims and a readiness to wage *jihad*. Mawdudi states that "those who are true to God, and those who reject Him, always stand against each other. The struggle between the 'bowed' ones and the 'rebels' is endless."[152] Muhammad ibn Dzhamil Zinu recommends unremitting hostility against those who deviate from Wahhabism:

> Bara'ah means enmity and hatred to those who contradict Allah, His Messenger (PBUH), the Companions of the Messenger (PBUH) and monotheistic believers; they include unbelievers, pagans and heretics, and inventors of *bid'ah* [innovations], who seek for healing, well-being, livelihood and directions not from Allah. One should love, treat benevolently and help every monotheistic believer who does not commit any actions forbidden by Shari'ah. And, on the contrary, as much as one can, one should detest, treat with enmity, and conduct *jihad* by word and heart against the one who breaks the Law of Allah, especially with those who look for help not from Allah.[153]

The founder of Wahhabism, Muhammad ibn Abd al-Wahhab, urges war against those who do not follow all the prescriptions of Islam:

> It is obligatory to fight with each group that refuses to fulfill the prescriptions of Islam until they start fulfilling them. Even if they recognize Allah and the Prophet Muhammad (PBUH) and fulfill some prescriptions of Islam, it is necessary to fight with them... If a group refuses to engage in *namaz* [prayer], fasting or undertake the Hajj, does not accept the prohibition to drink alcoholic beverages, does not accept the prohibition of marriage between close relatives, refuses to commit *jihad* against *kafirs* and does not fulfill religious obligations, a war shall be declared against this group even if they live in the same place.[154]

Ibn Dzhamil Zinu expresses the "us-versus-them" vision very vividly in the following passage:

> We should not love or be friends with those who have diverged from Islam under the pretext of nationalism, patriotism or, in particular, material consumer concerns imposed on us by the colonialist culture... We should find friends in Allah and choose enemies based on Allah. We should stand together with our Muslim brothers in all parts of the world, helping and protecting each other solidly and inviolately. We are obliged to be at enmity with those who encroach, harm and infringe upon the interests of our brothers, hindering them from living... The Islamic peoples, and particularly the Arabs, ought not to accept alien thoughts and ideas of different kinds, with which the peoples of materialistic Europe have to live. Such ideas are incompatible with the dignity of Muslims and do not correspond with the mission Allah entrusted to them... Being influenced by the practices of secular antireligious states and nations will lead to the loss by Muslims of their exclusive and high position, which was granted by Allah... Allah prohibited us from becoming like any other nation and any other people in their customs and slogans and even in clothing.[155]

Wahhabis instruct Muslims on the tactical details of conducting *jihad*. Abdurrahman Ben Nasyr as-Saadij calls for a thorough study of military issues in order to wage an effective *jihad*:

> People! Know that there are requirements in religion and *jihad*. There are requirements to be careful and conditions of how to fight against the enemy. These conditions will guarantee success... *Jihad* cannot be conducted without military knowledge and the experience of fighting a war. For *jihad*, it is necessary to increase power, to be resolute in issues of war, and to avoid losses... Now Muslims must... prepare for a war with enemies morally and materially and collect as much force as they are able. Today, a most important thing is to study the rules of war and military sciences. Then, Muslims will have a faithful, disciplined and well-prepared army. With its help, they will defend our religion and put in the proper place those who have overstepped. With this army, they will make the unbelievers tremble... For power can not be achieved without an army, force and energy.[156]

Dr. Yusus Ardaui defines the forms and conditions of *jihad*:

> Sabers and arrows conduct *jihad*. It can also be conducted by the pen
> or the tongue. *Jihad* can take the form of military battle as well as
> psychological, educational, humanitarian, economical and political
> forms. All these types of *jihad* need to be financially supported. Most
> important is the main requirement that they shall be 'for the cause of
> Allah.' They have to help Islam and spread its word worldwide."[157]

Sulayman ben Abdulaziz ad-Duwaysh stresses the need for proficiency in military matters: "Allah ordered believers to prepare armies, to know how to use modern technologies of war and how to fight with their enemies. Also, he obliged us to prepare and construct fortresses."[158]

In *Islamic Aqidah as Stated in the Holy Qur'an and Authentic Sunnah*, Muhammad ibn Dzhamil Zinu asks, "What is our duty towards Palestine, Lebanon, Afghanistan and other Muslim countries, which are waging *jihad*?" According to Zinu, this duty includes:

> Providing them with food, clothes, weapons and necessary means.
> Sending skilled propagandists to them to render assistance in solving
> their problems, consolidating their ranks, and explaining the *aqidah*
> of monotheism, so that they ask for help from Allah alone. Sending
> professional doctors in order to assist in treating the ill and wounded.
> Dispatching military experts, engineers and planning experts.
> Sending Muslim journalists, who can transmit accurate information.
> Sending volunteers who have expressed the desire to conduct *jihad*
> with their brothers. Observing closely and constantly all messages
> from the conflict areas, received from various information sources.
> Spreading information about the *mujahideen* through newspapers,
> magazines and other mass media outlets to unveil conspiracies against
> them, in order to attract attention to them and to make these plots
> fail. Revealing the existing Jewish danger in every possible way in
> Palestine, Lebanon and the Islamic world as a whole.[159]

According to the Wahhabi interpretation, peace is a temporary abstinence from obligatory *jihad* or armed struggle that has been enforced by circumstances: "Waging *jihad* depends on how possible it is." This rule is mentioned in such Wahhabi books as: *Islamic Aqidah according to the Holy Qur'an and Authentic*

Sunnah by Muhammad ibn Dzhamil Zinu; *Programs on Studies in Shari'ah Sciences: The Necessity to Observe the Sunnah of Allah's Messenger and Declaring Those who Deny it to be Apostates*" by Abd al-Aziz bin Baz; *Establishing the Laws of Allah* by M.A. Ibrahim, and others.[160]

TOLERANT HANAFI ISLAM VS. WAHHABISM

This Chapter will provide American politicians and journalists who are engaged in the battle of ideas with militant Islam with concrete advice on how the Qur'an, Sunnah, hadiths and other sources of Muslim theology may be used to refute the Wahhabi dogmas outlined in the previous Chapter. This Chapter presents the arguments and reasoning of Central Asian experts in Islamic affairs—imams of mosques, professors of Islamic educational establishments and scholars and leaders of Islamic theology. Their articles are published at the Web site of the American Foreign Policy Council, at <u>http://www.afpc.org</u>.

THE PROPRIETY OF THE WAHHABI INTERPRETATION OF ISLAM

All Central Asian experts in Islamic affairs refute the Wahhabis' right to interpret major Islamic ideas and the content of the Qur'an, Sunnah and hadiths without the consensus of the Islamic community and the most prominent and universally recognized *ulema*—Islamic experts in *tafsir* [the interpretation of holy texts]. According to Imam Rakhmatulla Hajji, the Wahhabis should not take upon themselves a role that does not belong to them, because Islamic doctrine states that "a man, believer in Allah and in the Doomsday, cannot become Imam of the community without the agreement of this community." Verse (28:83) of the Qur'anic Chapter "The Story" states: "(As for) that future abode, We assign it to those who have no desire to exalt themselves in the earth nor to make mischief and the good end is for those who guard (against evil)." This is also mentioned in the hadith of the Prophet Muhammad: "On the prohibition to strive for power and the preference to refuse the aspiration to govern, if (a person) has not been appointed or it is needed."

Abd al-Aziz bin Baz, one of Wahhabism's main ideologists, states: "One who violates openly or secretly shall know that he becomes an infidel and shall expect the possibility of murder or imprisonment."[161] However, according to Islamic law, it is first necessary to discover the true state of affairs and then to offer an apostate three chances to repent and to return to Islam.

The Wahhabis ignore this, instead labeling as "*takfir*" the officials of Islamic states as well as the law enforcement bodies and security agencies of these states.

Wahhabism belongs to Sunni Islam, which traditionally embraced four *mazhabs* or schools of thought. However, Wahhabis refuse to recognize the *mazhabs*, in order to claim the right to interpret Islamic dogmas in accordance with their political agenda. Refusal to join a *mazhab* is seen by Islamic experts as the most dangerous violation of the Islamic order. Wahhabis usually say, in their defense: "Allah and His Messenger Muhammad (PBUH) did not request us to follow any simple mortals or follow any *mazhab*." In response to them, one should point out the following verses of the Qur'an: "O, you who believe! Be careful of (your duty to) Allah and seek means of nearness to Him and strive hard in His way that you may be successful" (5:35); "...so ask the followers of the reminder if you do not know." (21:7)

It should be noted that, in Islamic tradition, one refers to different schools in Islam (*mazhabs*, schools of law, theological movements, Sufi *tarikats* [sects], and so on) by the name of their founder, irrespective of any evaluation of their theological, religious or legal content. However, those who consider Muhammad ibn Abd al-Wahhab their religious leader do not call themselves Wahhabis and even are offended to be referred to by such a name. They refer to themselves simply as Muslims (*muslimun*), monotheists (*muwahhidun*), or salafis, "followers of the beneficent ancestors," (*salafiyun*). They do not characterize as Wahhabism the teaching of Muhammad ibn Abd al-Wahhab or ideological movements that disseminate Wahhabi teachings or advocate Wahhabi positions.

The main reason why Wahhabis do not wish to be called Wahhabis is that although practically all Muslims are aware of the existence of heresy (*bid'ah*), not all Muslims are aware of whom an author and promoter of heresy might be. If the supporters of Wahhabism admit that they are Wahhabis, then logically they have to agree with accusations raised by Muslims against them—that, within the framework of Islam, Wahhabis are heretics. Muslims accuse Wahhabis of heresy because they do not follow the admonitions of the Prophet Muhammad but a religious school developed in the 18th Century (more than one thousand years after the death of the Prophet Muhammad) by someone who was a simple man, not an *alim*; that is, he was not a recognized expert in the teaching of the Prophet Muhammad.

One should take into consideration that the word "Wahhabi" in Arabic has different meaning, among them one of the names of Allah—Al-Wahhab (all-giving). Muhammad-Rasul Saaduev, the Chairman of Council of Religious Department of Muslims in Dagestan, issued the *fatwa*, "Can Muslims use the word 'Wahhabi?' It states that Muslims can apply the word "Wahhabi" to a follower of the teaching of Muhammad ibn Abd al-Wahhab. However, Muslims should not relate the word "Wahhabi" to one of the Names of Allah—Al-Wahhab (all-giving). Similarly, the words "Shafi'ite" and "Malikite" do not have a direct link with glorious names of Allah—Al-Malik (possessor) and Ash-Shafi'i (curing). These words originated from the names of the founders of the religious schools of thought of Imams Malik and Shafi'i. Imam Saaduev says there is not and there should not be anything in common between Wahhabis and a name of Allah, and that the activities of these people contradict the principles and dogmas of Islam.

HATRED AGAINST CHRISTIANS, JEWS, AND OTHER "INFIDELS"

Abdu Razzak, a Kyrgyz imam from the town of Cholpon-Ata, says in his sermons that Wahhabis

> advocate hatred towards Jews and Christians. However, the Prophet (PBUH) believed that Muslims, Jews and Christians—all are "People of the Book" and there should be peace and friendship among them. This is the desire of Allah! We must be, according to the Qur'an, "in the best relation with all People of the Book, with Jews and Christians." And we have to educate our children and inculcate a respect for Jews and Christians in their minds. We must understand the danger of illiteracy for our children, because this makes them easy targets for Wahhabis and Hizb-ut-Tahrir. Our children must respect knowledge.[162]

According to Imam Rakhmatulla Hajji, the Wahhabi characterization of Jews and Christians as disbelievers radically contradicts Islamic doctrine. According to the Qur'an, Jews and Christians are "People of the Holy Book" (*ahl al-Kitab*), since the books of revelation were sent from Allah to different religious communities: the Torah to Moses, psalms to David, and the Gospel to Jesus. All Qur'anic prophets were monotheists; therefore, the term "hanif"—professing true monotheism—has been used to refer to them. In Islam, there is no difference between the messages God sent to different prophets. A famous and important Qur'anic verse (2:136) which Wahhabis avoid mentioning states: "Say: We believe in Allah and (in) that which had been revealed to us, and (in) that which was revealed to Ibrahim and Ishmael and Ishaq and Yaqoub and the tribes, and (in) that which was given to Musa [Moses] and Isa [Jesus], and (in) that which was given to the prophets from their Lord, we do not make any distinction between any of them, and to Him do we submit."

The legal status of the "People of the Holy Book" and people of other religions and the relationship of Muslims with them is regulated by *fiqh*—Muslim jurisprudence. According to the Muslim jurisprudence, all the "ahl al-Kitab" [the "People of the Holy Book"], i.e. Jews and Christians, are under the protection of the Muslim community. From the early stages of Islam, the conditions of the "People of the Holy Book" who lived in Islamic countries were more favorable than the conditions of people of non-Christian religions who lived in European countries during the Middle Age. Very often, Jews and Eastern Orthodox Christians preferred to live under the rule of Muslims rather under the rule of West European Christian Catholic authorities. The "People of the Book" were a significant part of the administrative apparatus of the caliphate and played an active role in its economic life, especially as craftsmen and traders.

There is another important verse (109:1-6) of the Qur'anic Chapter "Al-*Kafir*un" ("Disbelievers"), which states: "In the name of Allah, the Beneficent, the Merciful. Say: O unbelievers! I do not serve that which you serve, Nor do you serve Him Whom I serve: Nor am I going to serve that which you serve, Nor are you going to serve Him Whom I serve: You shall have your religion and I shall have my religion." The above mentioned verses of the Qur'an and the concept of "ahl al-Kitab" based on them provide a theological basis to justify peaceful relations between Muslims and Christians and Jews, as well as between Muslim countries and the rest of the world.

Wahhabis claim that Arabs are the best Muslims, first of all because they know the original language of the Qur'an. However, according to Imam Rakhmatulla Hajji:

> ...the Prophet (PBUH) said, "There is no supremacy of an Arab over non-Arab...;" "all people are equal, as are the comb's teeth." The Prophet Muhammad (PBUH) in his hadiths repeatedly said that he was sent by Allah to all people.[163] The existence of people of different nationalities is stipulated by God's will and wisdom. As

it is emphasized in the *ayah* [verse] (30:22) of the Qur'anic *surah* [Chapter], the difference of people in languages and skin colors is the essence of "God's sign." "And one of His signs is the creation of the heavens and the earth and the diversity of your tongues and colors." The ethnic and religious diversity of people is not a reason for factionalism; it was God's will, mentioned in the *ayah* (49:13) of the Qur'anic *Surah*: "O you men! surely We have created you of a male and a female, and made you tribes and families that you may know each other..." Diversity should be the source not of factionalism, but rather of competitiveness in the service of the common good, as it is stated in the *ayah* (5:48) of the Qur'anic *Surah*: "For every one of you did We appoint a law and a way, and if Allah had pleased He would have made you (all) a single people, but that He might try you in what He gave you, therefore strive with one another to hasten to virtuous deeds; to Allah is your return, of all (of you), so He will let you know that in which you differed ..."

Vladimir Soloviev, a Russian authority on Islam, wrote that "[f]rom the texts of the Qur'an, we may see how unfair were reproaches made towards Muhammad, accusing him of fanaticism, intolerance, and professing religious violence. In the Holy Book, there is no single dictum that shows Muhammad's deliberate abuse of religion."[164] According to Muhammad, holy war was a temporarily needed measure rather than a permanent undertaking.

The Ottoman Empire followed the norms of Muslim law with regard to Jews and Christians. The traditionally tolerant attitude of the empire's authorities towards the Jews existed even when Sultan Abdul Hamid II (1842-1918) cancelled the first Ottoman Constitution of 1876 and established a dictatorship throughout the empire. According to one scholar: "In general, the most tolerant towards the followers of other religions were the followers of the Hanafi school of thought; the cruelest were the followers of the Hanbali school of thought, especially the followers of Wahhabism, who advocated all kinds of innovations that have no substantiation in the Qur'an and Sunnah."[165]

In Abdu Razzak's sermons, he relates the following story from the hadiths:

> The Prophet Muhammad (PBUH) would sit with his disciples in his house when a Jewish funeral procession passed by. The Prophet (PBUH) stood up and remained standing until the entire procession passed. His disciples asked him why he showed such a respect to a Jewish funeral procession. He answered, "Allah said in the Qur'an that he had created all human beings as super living creatures. I stood up to pay my respect to the son of a human being." We must respect all people. Our presence on the earth is just a short stop in the shadow of a tree on the eternal hard path of life under a hot, burning sun. We must respect everyone whom we happen to meet during this short stop in the shadow of a tree.[166]

HATRED TOWARD OTHER MUSLIMS WHO DO NOT SHARE THEIR INTERPRETATION OF ISLAM

One of the main postulates of Wahhabism states that Muslims who do not believe in the main dogmas of the Wahhabi doctrine are disbelievers and apostates, against whom the use of violence and *jihad* (holy war) is not only permitted but is an obligation of each of the "faithful." As Imam Razzak points out, this postulate violates two of the fundamental provisions of the Qur'an—the prohibition against declaring *jihad* against brothers in faith and the prohibition to doubt the sincerity of belief on the part of a Muslim until Allah, on the Day of Judgment, makes His decision on the genuineness of a person's faith: "In *surah* 3, *ayah* 9, Allah says that all Muslims are brothers. They have one father—Adam, and one mother—Eve. Muslim cannot wish to commit evil against other Muslims."[167]

Another verse of the Qur'an (49:10) states: "The believers are but brethren, therefore, make peace between your brethren..." Among the statements of God retold by the Prophet Muhammad was the following: "O, My servants, I have forbidden myself and also you to oppress, therefore, do not oppress each other."[168] The Prophet also said, "Speaking evil of a Muslim is (an expression of) dishonesty and fighting with him is (witness of) disbelief."[169] (Al-Bukhari; Muslim). The Prophet Muhammad also said: "The life, honesty and property of (other) Muslims shall be inviolable for every Muslim."[170]

Wahhabis assert that the slightest deviation from monotheism turns a Muslim into a "disbeliever." This person then becomes an apostate; his or her life and property are no longer inviolate, and he or she can be killed and his or her property seized. However, according to Imam Rakhmatulla Hajji, a reliable hadith of the Prophet (PBUH) states: "A Muslim is a brother to a Muslim: he doesn't oppress him, nor turns him down, nor deceives or despises him... A real evil for a man is to despise his Muslim brother. Everything is inviolable in Islam for another Muslim: his blood, his property and his honor."[171]

Wahhabi ideologists state in some of their booklets and brochures that "if a Muslim doesn't consider polytheists, Jews, Christians, atheists, sorcerers and others to be disbelievers, he becomes a disbeliever himself." However, Shari'ah forbids Muslims to "scold a believer with the word disbelief" and actions of this kind.[172]

According Imam Muslim Hajji, a person's faith is not perfect until he wishes the same things for other people that he wishes for himself, and until he behaves towards others as he wishes that others should behave towards him. If a human heart contains hatred towards a Muslim, it means that the faith of this person is weak; this person is in danger, and his heart is vicious and not ready to meet Allah.

Wahhabism has consistently been used for military-political purposes, such as the religious justification of military campaigns and the use of violence against the Muslim neighbors of the Saudi dynasty. This is a breach of another fundamental norm of the Qur'an—namely, the prohibition against using violent measures in religion. A famous verse (2:256) of the Qur'an says: "Let there be no compulsion in religion. Truth stands out clear from Error..." Islam teaches that conversion must be done on the basis of conviction, not force.

HATRED AGAINST WESTERN DEMOCRACY, CULTURE AND WAY OF LIFE

According to Imam Rakhmatulla Hajji, it is groundless to speak about Western democracy as a threat to Islam and about the alleged bankruptcy of the Western system. The concept of democracy is multifaceted, and Islamic norms perfectly fit into it. Islam legitimizes democracy; the Qur'an does not authorize any intermediaries or monarchs as anointed sovereigns. There is no contradiction between democracy and Islam.

The Qur'an considers pluralism to be God's predetermined will. According to the Qur'an, the diversity in the world is caused by God's will and wisdom. As *ayah* 30:22 emphasizes: "And one of His signs is the creation of the heavens and the earth and the diversity of your tongues and colors; most surely there are signs in this for the learned." In other words, educated people will recognize distinctions among people in languages and skin colors as one aspect of "God's sign."

According to Islam, mankind was originally a single race and an indivisible spiritual community, but God wished to split up people into different tribes, peoples, and religions:

- Qur'anic *ayah* 2:213: "(All) people are a single nation; so Allah raised prophets as bearers of good news and as warners, and He revealed with them the Book with truth, that it might judge between people in that in which they differed; and none but the very people who were given it differed about it after clear arguments had come to them, revolting among themselves; so Allah has guided by His will those who believe to the Truth about which they differed; and Allah guides whom He pleases to the right path."

- Qur'anic *ayah* 49:13: "O you men! Surely We have created you of a male and a female, and made you tribes and families that you may know each other; surely the most honorable of you with Allah is the one among you most careful (of his duty)."

Neither ethnic nor religious pluralism, which we witness in democratic political systems, deviates from God's norms and neither should be condemned. Diversity is a source of competitive spirit in service of the general welfare, not a source for conflict. Qur'anic *ayah* 5:48 says: "For every one of you did We appoint a law and a way, and if Allah had pleased He would have made you (all) a single people, but that He might try you in what he gave you, therefore strive with one another to hasten to virtuous deeds; to Allah is your return, of all (of you), so He will let you know that in which you differed."

True Islam believes that pluralism promotes universal solidarity, harmony and mutual enrichment. Qur'anic *ayah* 49:13 says: "O you men! Surely We have created you of a male and a female, and made you tribes and families that you may know each other; surely the most honorable of you with Allah is the one among you most careful (of his duty)."

According to Imam Rakhmatulla Hajji, Islam rejects any isolation—economic, intellectual, ethnic or cultural. In order to deepen mutual understanding with other communities, Muslims need to carry on a dialogue with them, especially with "the People of the Book," Christians and Jews. Such inter-religious and intercultural dialogue should be kindhearted, positive and constructive. Qur'anic *ayah* 29:46 says: "And do not dispute with the followers of the Book… and say: We believe in that which has been revealed to us and revealed to you, and our God and your God is One, and to Him do we submit."

True Islam proclaims freedom of worship, a core principle of the democratic political system. If a pluralism of faiths was designed by God, then, according to Imam Rakhmatulla Hajji, Wahhabi attempts to abolish it are illegal and senseless. In particularly, it is futile to advocate a mandatory unification of people under the banner of a single religion—Islam. In the Qur'anic *ayah* 10:99, God addresses the Prophet Muhammad with such an exhortation: "And if your Lord had pleased, surely all those who are in the earth would have believed, all of them; will you then force men till they become believers?" Another Qur'anic *ayah* (28:56) reminds Prophet Muhammad: "Surely you cannot guide whom you love, but Allah guides whom He pleases." Qur'anic *ayah* (12:103) says: "And most men will not believe though you desire it eagerly."

The Qur'an confirms freedom of religious choice dozens of times, condemning any attempts to violate it. The duty of the Islamic Prophet Muhammad, as well as other prophets, is not to force people to accept Islam but only to deliver God's message truly and clearly. (See Qur'anic *ayah*s 5:99; 16:35; 24:54; 29:18; 36:17). "Nothing is (incumbent) on the Apostle but to deliver (the message)." God directs the Prophet Muhammad in Qur'anic *ayah*s 88:21-22: "Therefore do remind, for you are only a Reminder. You are not a watcher over them." Qur'anic *ayah* 2:256 confirms, with the utmost clarity, the principle of nonviolence in religious questions: "There is no compulsion in religion."

The tolerant Islam of Central Asia presumes that true faith stems from an internal desire, and cannot be inserted into a human heart by force. A human being is granted freedom of choice, and he or she has responsibility for his or her beliefs. Qur'anic *ayah* 17:15 says: "Whoever goes aright, for his own soul does he go aright; and whoever goes astray, to its detriment only does he go astray." Besides, God himself will resolve peoples' disagreements concerning faith on Doomsday. Qur'anic *ayah* 22:17 says: "Surely those who believe and those who are Jews and the Sabeans and the Christians and the Magians and those who associate (others with Allah)—surely Allah will decide between them on the Day of Resurrection; surely Allah is a witness over all things." Thus, religious divergences will be sorted out when divine justice is dispensed.

According to Imam Rakhmatulla Hajji, one of the main Wahhabi claims is the "indisputable right of the Muslim clergy to rule the state." But, Islamic law, Shari'ah, is not fully applied in any state in the world. It may be a basic source of legislation and of constitutions in some Islamic countries, but the actual laws in most Muslim countries are still secular in essence. In order to support their concept of the "non-recognition of any power that diverges from the instructions of Shari'ah," the Wahhabis most often cite the Qur'anic *ayah* 4:59, which says: "Oh you who believe! Obey Allah and obey the Apostle and those in authority from among you." This Qur'anic *ayah* is distorted by them because they only cite half of it. The second part of this Qur'anic *ayah* continues, "then if you quarrel about anything, refer it to Allah and the Apostle." Omitting the second part makes it possible for people—not Allah or the Apostle—to deal with the quarrel. Arabic Wahhabi groups use this method in order to justify monarchical rule in their countries. The Wahhabis present this Qur'anic verse as a categorical order to not obey "unbelievers" who are in power. But this Qur'anic verse does not criticize democracy and it can be applied to secular states with a predominately Muslim population.

Wahhabis devote a great deal of attention to the establishment of an Islamic state—the "caliphate." They refer to the Qur'an, which, they believe, justifies the establishment of a caliphate in four places:

- *Surah 6, ayah* 133 says, "If He pleases, He may take you off, and make whom He pleases successors after you, even as He raised you up from the seed of another people."

- *Surah 7, ayah* 129 states, "He said: It may be that your Lord will destroy your enemy and make you rulers in the land, then He will see how you act."

- *Surah 11, ayah* 57 says, "And my Lord will bring another people in your place, and you cannot do Him any harm."

- *Surah 24, ayah* 55 reads, "Allah has promised to those of you who believe and do good that He will most certainly make them rulers in the earth as He made rulers those before them, and that He will most certainly establish for them their religion which He has chosen for them, and that He will most certainly, after their fear, give them security in exchange; they shall serve Me, not associating aught with Me; and whoever is ungrateful after this, these it is who are the transgressors."

However, responsible and respected Islamic religious authorities argue that the era of the caliphate has passed. Allah does not force Muslims to create a caliphate. There is no such instruction in the above mentioned *ayah*s of the Qur'an. According to Islamic religious authorities, the first three above mentioned *ayah*s only say that one generation of people will disappear, and another generation of people will replace them. The fourth *ayah* has a more explicit political meaning, and the Wahhabis mostly refer to this fourth *ayah*. However, in order to understand this *ayah*, one should know its background. The context is that despite the fact that the Prophet Muhammad moved from Mecca to Medina, he could not escape the enmity of the mushriks, the polytheists; war with them was going on constantly. He had to carry his sword day and night. One of those days, a *sahaba*[173] addressed him: "Messenger of Allah! Will we carry our swords up to the end of days or will peace come some day?" The Prophet answered, "Have a little patience. The time will come, when you, being in a very big community, will go around without arms." The fourth *ayah* applied to the Prophet Muhammad's followers at that time.

Kinsanbay hajji Abdurahmanov believes that:

> ...in Central Asia, there is not the slightest chance to create a caliphate. Most Arab countries had been part of the earlier Islamic caliphate. It was their great-great-grandfathers who helped the British and French colonialists to divide the soil of the caliphate into the different states and it is first of all the Arabs, not the citizens of Central Asia, who should be obliged to recreate the caliphate if that is what they wish to do. But the people in Arab countries are not going to do this, in part because people of different faiths live in Arab countries and it is necessary to reckon with them. So, why should we give our lands to the caliphate if the Arabs do not? Kyrgyzstan is a Muslim country and many Muslims live here, but we are not going to become a part of an Islamic caliphate.[174]

He continues:

> The [Wahhabi] representatives of Hizb-ut-Tahrir have distributed leaflets among people in which it was written that true Muslims should live in a caliphate. But if we follow their logic, members of Hizb-ut-Tahrir themselves are not true Muslims because they do not live in a caliphate. Now these Wahhabis say that if you do not live at least 30 days in a caliphate, you can not be a true Muslim, you will be expelled from the Muslim community, and you will not be admitted to Paradise.

> But there are no such ideas in the Qur'an. The Prophet (PBUH) never made such claims. If Allah had placed such conditions on Muslims, the Prophet (PBUH) would have necessarily communicated God's will on this subject. The Prophet (PBUH) related everything that Allah told him, but the Prophet (PBUH) never said that the caliphate would exist forever. Every Muslim lives how and where he or she lives now. A Muslim caliphate does not currently exist anywhere. Muslims live in various countries, under different laws, and many possess many rights. According to Qur'an, there should not be any compulsion in questions of religion. Why should a Muslim take weapons in hand in

order to force a caliphate upon others? If people do not wish to create a caliphate, one should not force them to do this.[175]

WAHHABI SUPPRESSION OF WOMEN

The following *ayah* (4:34) is used by Wahhabis to demonstrate the alleged inequality of men and women, "Men are the maintainers of women because Allah has made some of them to excel others and because they spend out of their property." They interpret this *ayah* as if men have a higher status than women. However, according to Mullah Zakir Hajji, most famous commentators on the Qur'an interpret this *ayah* as follows, "Men are the trustees of their wives, because Allah has made some of them to excel others and because they spend out of their property."[176] In the opinion of a famous *tafsir*[177] expert of the Qur'an, this *ayah* communicates the idea that men and women complement each other and are inseparably linked, and just because men own property does not mean women are inferior.

In contrast, the tolerant Hanafi school of Sunni Islam takes a much different position on the proper role of women in society. According to Mullah Zakir Hajji, Islam pays special attention to women, insuring their honor and proper status in a society. The Qur'an emphasizes that Allah has created all living creatures, including human beings, in pairs: "He has created you from a single being, and then made its mate of the same (kind)…" *ayah* (39:6); "He made mates for you from among yourselves…" *ayah* (42:11); "He is Who created you from a single being, and of the same (kind) did He make his mate, that he might incline to her…" *ayah* (7:189); "And one of His signs is that He created mates for you from yourselves that you may find rest in them, and He put between you love and compassion; most surely there are signs in this for a people who reflect." *ayah* (30:21). Islam states that man and woman complement each other and are a mean for mutual perfection of each other: "They are an apparel for you and you are an apparel for them." *ayah* (2:187).

The Qur'an grants special protection to women, who are more vulnerable than men: "Surely those who accuse chaste believing women, unaware (of the evil), are cursed in this world and the hereafter, and they shall have a grievous chastisement. On the day when their tongues and their hands and their feet shall bear witness against them as to what they did." *ayah*s (24:23-24)

Islam carefully stipulates women's rights in marriage. According to Shari'ah, marriage should be for life; and both man and woman should declare their consent in the presence of two witnesses. However, the Wahhabis do not follow these rules. For example, after observing the behavior of Wahhabis in the Karategin zone of Tajikistan, Kudratulla hajji Abdurahmanov ascertained that Wahhabis have the following types of marriage. The first one is "marriage for the time being" or "temporary marriage." When arriving at a certain location, Wahhabis can get married temporarily. Upon leaving, the marriage is dissolved. The second type is marriage for a sum of money, in which a set amount of money is agreed upon for a Wahhabi to spend for living expenses in a common marriage. The third type is a one-time marriage, when a Wahhabi consorts with a woman for one or two days. As a formality, a Wahhabi can obtain consent from a lady for this type of marriage. All these types of marriages are forbidden in Islam.

The tolerant Hanafi school of Sunni Islam believes that both genders have the opportunity for a decent human existence on Earth. They both have the right to own property and to dispose of it as they wish, including by sale, purchase, pledge, a bequeath for charity purposes, and so on. Champions of the Hanafi school cite following *ayah*s to justify their point of view:

- *Ayah* (4:7) : "Men shall have a portion of what the parents and the near relatives leave, and women shall have a portion of what the parents and the near relatives leave, whether there is little or much of it; a stated portion."

- *Ayah* (4:32): "Men shall have (their) portion of what they have earned, and women shall have (their) portion of what they have earned…"

Men and women will equally be rewarded according to their deeds:

- *Ayah* (4:124): "And whoever does good deeds whether male or female and he (or she) is a believer—these shall enter the garden, and they shall not be dealt with a jot unjustly."

- *Ayah* (16:97): "Whoever does good whether male or female and he is a believer, We will most certainly make him live a happy life, and We will most certainly give them their reward for the best of what they did."

- *Ayah* (40:40): "Whoever does good, whether male or female, and he is a believer, these shall enter the garden, in which they shall be given sustenance without measure."

- *Ayah* (9:71): "The believing men and the believing women, they are guardians of each other…"

- *Ayah* (47:19): "Allah asks the Holy Prophet for protection for your fault and for the believing men and the believing women."

THE WAHHABI INTERPRETATION OF HOLY WAR— *JIHAD*

The word *jihad* became familiar to Americans and Europeans as a term for the terrorist activities performed by Wahhabis and others with similar attitudes. However, Islam traditionally considers "*jihad*" not primarily as waging war but as the peaceful and constructive efforts of believers to achieve moral self-perfection. According to Mullah Zakir Hajji, the word "*jihad*" is one of the most incorrectly understood Islamic terms. Its original meaning is "endeavor," "diligence," or "struggle." *Jihad* in Islam means any effort that a Muslim undertakes in order to live according to the commands of Allah. This word can also mean "an armed struggle" if it is waged by the rules of Islam. Originally, this term was understood as a struggle to protect Islam. The best *jihad*, in the broader sense, is to be honest, sincere, and to always speak the truth. Allah has given freedom of opinion and choice to Muslims. But He ordered everyone to speak the truth. This is one of the best ways to conduct *jihad*. The Islamic pundit Abu Dawud at-Tirmizi cites the Prophet Muhammad, who said: "The best *jihad* is (saying) a just word in the presence of unjust ruler."[178] He also said: "The one who cares about a widow and the poor is similar to a fighter on the way of Allah"[179].

According to Imam Abdumutalib Hajji, the former chief Mufti of Kyrgyzstan, Islam does not permit Muslims to kill innocent and defenseless people. The Qur'an states, "Allah does not forbid you respecting those who have not made war against you on account of (your) religion, and have not driven you forth from your homes." *ayah* (60:8). The Qur'an also says, "And you will certainly find the nearest in friendship to those who believe (to be) those who say: We are Christians." *ayah* (5:82).

In order to justify terrorism, the Wahhabis cite only partial verses from the Qur'an, distorting their meaning, such as: "Slay the idolaters wherever you find them…" and "O Prophet! Strive hard against the unbelievers and the hypocrites and be unyielding to them…" (9:5, 73). One should consider and understand every verse of the Qur'an in its full context and take into consideration the concrete historic situation when the Qur'anic texts were revealed. The complete content of the above verse states: "So when the Sacred Months have passed away, then *slay the idolaters wherever you find them*, and take them captives and besiege them and lie in wait for them in every ambush, then if they repent and keep up prayer and pay the poor-rate, leave their way free to them; surely Allah is Forgiving, Merciful." The 9th Chapter, from which this verse is taken from, addresses how Muslims should deal with an enemy who breaks an agreement and does not keep his word. The verse also states that only after four months and if another party has not renounced its malicious intents, can military actions against this party be renewed.

The historic background of this *ayah* is well known. The events occurred during the times of early Islam, when the Prophet Muhammad sent a group of Muslims, led by Abu Bakr, to hajj (pilgrimage to Mecca) in accordance with the temporary "Hudaybiya agreement" he had concluded with the inhabitants of Mecca. But Mecca's idolaters broke the agreement, according to which they should not have hindered Muslims from making the pilgrimage. They became aggressive, and attempted to destroy the Islamic religion completely, forcing the Prophet to annul his agreement with them and the Muslim community to prepare to protect itself.

According to Imam Abdumutalib Hajji, the former chief Mufti of Kyrgyzstan , the Qur'an implies that even while waging a war, Muslims should not exceed the framework permitted for military actions (i.e., they should strictly follow the established rules of waging a war). This commandment does not apply to war against all idolaters, but only to those who, like the inhabitants of Mecca at the time, have repeatedly broken agreements with Muslims and attacked them again and again. Nevertheless, according to Islam, Muslims must give idolaters an opportunity to think twice about their aggressive actions against Muslims. Also, according to fundamental Qur'anic commandments, it is prohibited to require that defeated idolaters adopt Islam: "There is no compulsion in religion." *ayah* (2:256). It is forbidden to force defeated idolaters to make a choice between "conversion to Islam or death." Military actions are allowed only for defense and should be stopped if opponents renounce their malicious intentions and abandon their aggression, according to *ayah*s 2:192, 193.

Moreover, the sixth *ayah* of the ninth *surah* states, "And if one of the idolaters seek protection from you, grant him protection till he hears the word of Allah, then make him attain his place of safety, this is because they are a people who do not know." *ayah* (9:6) It is obvious here that Islam aspires to save everyone and treat people properly, no matter to which faith they belong. Thus, the year 630, when the campaign on Tabuk started, was called "the year of embassies." During this year, almost all Arabian tribes joined the Muslims. In addition, in this year the Muslims reached an agreement with Christians, according to which the latter had to pay an annual tax (jizya) in exchange for the Muslims' patronage and protection. The Jewish tribes and representatives of other religious communities agreed to these conditions as well, under which all of them retained their freedom of worship.

The Wahhabis also interpret the following Sunnah of the Prophet in a perverted way in order to advocate the application of force: "If someone from you sees *something forbidden by Shari'ah*, change it by your hand, and if you cannot make it by your hand, *stop the sin* by your tongue, and if you cannot—then *at least* by your heart, and *this will be the weakest demonstration of belief.*"[180] In the authentic hadiths, the text appears in the following way: "The one from you, who sees *a misdeed*, should change it by your hand, and *if you are not able to do it*, then—by your tongue, and if you are not able to do it—then by your heart, this is the *weakest degree of belief.*"[181] This Sunnah refers to observing the norms of Shari'ah within the Muslim ummah. And there is no direct or indirect call to violence.

According to Mullah Zakir Hajji:

> The Prophet (PBUH) taught that war is not a reason to forget about mercy: "Be afraid of the prayer of an offended one, for no obstacle between it and Allah exists." Thus, the Messenger of Allah (PBUH) does not distinguish between offended believers and unbelievers. While

carrying out military operations, Islam forbids killing civilians. The Qur'anic *ayah* (9:6) says, "And if one of the idolaters seeks protection from you, grant him protection till he hears the word of Allah, then make him attain his place of safety." The Qur'an (4:90) also instructs, "Therefore if they withdraw from you and do not fight you and offer you peace, then Allah has not given you a way against them."

Abduhafiz Abdujabar points out:

> The Holy Qur'an is the only law we obey in our deeds and actions, and it bans killing. Many verses contain unambiguous instructions banning the killing of living creatures unless you have a right or just reason to do so. For example, the Qur'an says, 'Do not kill a soul unless having the right. Allah has prohibited it.' (17:33).

> What does it mean "unless having the right?" This means killing is permitted only for capital crimes as defined by Shari'ah. The terrorist killer does not know who will be the victim of his insane actions; he does not know who will lose his life as a result of his deeds. So, how can he know whether his victims deserve death by a blind act of execution? There are many Qur'anic verses that impart the same message. One of them states, "And if somebody kills a believer deliberately, than the requital to him (the murderer) is hell, where he will dwell forever. Allah will get angry with him, condemn him and make a great punishment for him." *ayah* (4:93) This verse makes it is obvious that a person who kills someone else without a good reason will be condemned to Hell.[182]

Muslims should not kill old people, women, and children. Imam al-Bukhari cites the following hadith in his book *Sahih Bukhari*: When, after a battle, a murdered woman had been found, the Prophet (PBUH) condemned this murder, saying, "She did not fight."[183] Women and children should not be hurt if they do not take part in military operations. Later, this rule was developed further, when Muhammad gave instructions to his armies, military leaders, and caliphs. Furthermore, this rule is included in "Shari'ah's Norms of Waging War" (*ghazwah*). The hadith says, "…truly, Allah will show His mercy only to the merciful ones from His slaves."[184] Another hadith also says, "Indeed Allah loves (demonstrations of) kindness in everything."[185]

According to Mullah Zakir Hajji, armed *jihad* is the personal religious duty of the believer as long as it is waged within a legal framework. *Jihad* can be treated as holy war for the protection of religious freedom, the fatherland, relatives, loved ones, and one's home only in the case of an armed attack and aggression.

The greatest 19th Century European specialist on Islam, Reinhardt Dozy, wrote:

> The Qur'an does not contain any order that would direct Muslims to launch a war against all unbelievers... Holy war becomes a duty only in that unique instance when the enemies of Islam happen to attack; if somebody understands the instructions of the Qur'an differently, then this is the fault of the voluntary interpretations of theologians.[186]

According to Mullah Zakir Hajji, the principles of tolerance and pluralism of the Qur'an are incompatible with an offensive war waged for establishing the faith, which presupposes violence against believers of other faiths and against unbelievers. Any aggressive war is unacceptable in Islam. According to Islam, if no one declares war on Muslims or their religion, and if no one invades their territory, Muslims have no right to kill. The Qur'an's verse 2:190 says, "And struggle in the way of Allah with those who struggle with you, and do not exceed the limits, surely Allah does not love those who exceed the limits."

A war with non-Muslims is possible only as resistance to aggression, and not as a way to expand spheres of influence, or to impose the Wahhabis' understanding of Islam as the only true interpretation of Islamic values. The Qur'an instructs, "And struggle with them until there is no persecution, and religion should be only for Allah, but if they desist, then there should be no hostility except against the oppressors." *ayah* (2:193)

Surah 9, which allows a declaration of war on pagans, precisely emphasizes that this rule is not applied to those idolaters who have not broken peace arrangements with Muslims: "So as long as they are true to you, be true to them; surely Allah loves those who are careful (of their duty)." *ayah* (9:7) The Qur'an also stipulates, "Allah does not forbid you respecting those who have not made war against you on account of (your) religion, and have not driven you forth from your homes, that you show them kindness and deal with them justly; surely Allah loves the doers of justice." *ayah* (60:8) Famous Islamic commentators on this *ayah* consider that the phrase "Allah does not forbid you..." is an admonition that "even in relation to unbelievers we should be friendly and fair, if they do not aspire to destroy our faith; the Prophet showed this to us by his own example;" "justice in its absolute sense is a duty towards all creations of Allah, regardless of what religious faith they believe, friendliness prescribed by this *ayah* is applied to the representatives of all faiths and religions who do not wage wars with Muslims because of their religion, and such instruction cannot be cancelled by any other *ayah*."[187] The Qur'an also declares, "And you will certainly find the nearest in friendship to those who believe (to be) those who say: We are Christians." *ayah* (5:82).

According to Mullah Zakir Hajji, the terrorist acts that al-Qaeda committed on September 11, 2001 in the United States—and earlier in other countries of the world—have nothing to do with the acts of righteous Muslims. According to Islamic doctrine, whoever kills at least one person should be considered the murderer of all mankind: "Whoever slays a soul, unless it be for manslaughter or for mischief in the land, it is as though he slew all men; and whoever keeps it alive, it is as though he kept alive all men." *ayah* (5:32) Islam does not contain any justification for terrorism, violence or oppression. In fact, the Prophet Muhammad said, "Where there is violence, there is no Islam."

According to Mullah Zakir Hajji, Islam has established the rule of *fatwa* announcements, which proclaim religious-legal conclusions, including on the subject of when it is appropriate to declare *jihad*. The Wahhabis, who call on Muslims to wage *jihad* against some states or peoples, ignore this rule, which states that only *alim*s (Islamic scholars and theologians), who possess profound knowledge of the Islamic sciences and Shari'ah and who are recognized by the whole Muslim world, have the right to make such pronouncements. The Wahhabis have no right to declare *jihad* for the following reasons:

First of all, the founder of Wahhabism, Muhammad ibn Abd al-Wahhab was not an *alim*. The *fatwa*, "Is it possible to call Muhammad ibn Abd al-Wahhab an *alim*?" states:

> *Alim*s are the people who possess knowledge of Islam and strictly carry out all the instructions of Allah. *Alim*s recognize the Holy Qur'an, hadiths and all four Islamic schools of thought. Muhammad ibn Abd al-Wahhab did not recognize the legitimacy of the four schools of

thought, made his own comments on *ayah*s of the Holy Qur'an and hadiths of the Prophet Muhammad (PBUH), rejected the opinions of other *alim*s and the Muslim ummah, and respected only his own understanding of Islam. Muhammad ibn Abd al-Wahhab criticized the companions of the Prophet (peace be upon them) and distorted their judgments. He rejected hadiths that honored the Companions of the Prophet (peace be upon them). In doing this, he ignored the directions of the Prophet Muhammad (PBUH), who taught us, 'Follow my companions (peace be upon them), they will direct you to the right way.'

The biggest mistake of Muhammad ibn Abd al-Wahhab was that he labeled as *kafirs* (disbelievers) all those who refused to follow his ideology. In doing so, he once again rejected the directions of the Prophet (PBUH), who stated, "The one who calls a Muslim a *kafir* shows disbelief towards the Almighty." Obviously, Muhammad ibn Abd al-Wahhab was not an *alim*, since the true *alim* strives to help other people take the right track. Instead, Muhammad ibn Abd al-

Wahhab led his followers astray. His doctrine contradicts the Holy Qur'an and hadiths, and caused dangerous negative processes in the ummah and generated enmity and contention among Muslims.[188]

Secondly, according to the Islamic scholar Sayyid Afandi Chirkeysky, Wahhabis are a lost people who delude others; the Islamic world does not recognize them as *alim*s, therefore their conclusions cannot have legal force.[189] Wahhabis impose their opinions, which do not comply with Shari'ah, on Muslims, and at the same time ignore the edicts of authoritative Islamic scholars. Osama bin Laden, in his first interview after the September 11th attacks, given to the Pakistani journalist Hamid Mir, declared: "The *fatwa* of any official *alim* does not mean anything to me."

Abduhafiz Abdujabar points out:

The Qur'an and hadiths of the Prophet (PBUH) unambiguously condemn suicide. Knowledge of the Qur'an and the hadiths makes it clear that young people who kill themselves will never become martyrs and will never gain a reward in the other world alongside prophets and upright people. Such an expectation has no grounding in Islam, and no sensible Muslim will accept it. The Holy Qur'an clearly and explicitly states, "Do not kill yourself. Allah was (will be) merciful to you." (4:29)

People may commit suicide if they find themselves in difficult financial, physical or emotional circumstances. But they should not do this because God is merciful. Muslims should not lose hope, should not believe that life is over, and that God will not help them. So it is said in the Holy Qur'an. There are also several hadiths that instruct us. For example, we read in al-Bukhari: "One who killed himself by any weapon will be tortured by the same weapon in hell." The meaning is clear: one who kills himself with a knife will be tortured by a knife; one who suffocates himself will be punished by suffocation. Al-Bukhari also cites another hadith: "One who suffocates himself (hangs himself) will be hung; one who pierces himself (by a sharp weapon), will be pierced," i.e. the method used to commit suicide in this world will be the same method used for his torture in the other world.[190]

THE BATTLE OF IDEAS IN THE MASS MEDIA

Military victories in Iraq and Afghanistan do little to alleviate continued U.S. defeats on the most important front in the War on Terror—the battle of ideas. Back in 2003, the Advisory Group on Public Diplomacy for the Arab and Muslim World, a subcommittee of the U.S. Advisory Commission on Public Diplomacy created to provide oversight of U.S. attempts to understand, inform, and influence foreign publics, issued a report that stated:

> America has not excelled in the struggle of ideas in the Arab and Muslim world. As the director of the Pew Research Center said earlier this year, attitudes toward the United States "have gone from bad to worse."

> Hostility toward America has reached shocking levels. Again, according to Pew, "the bottom has fallen out of Arab and Muslim support for the United States"... The Arab and Muslim world, however, cannot be addressed in isolation. Animosity toward the U.S. is part of a broader crisis worldwide.

> What is required is not merely tactical adaptation but strategic, and radical, transformation.[191]

More than three years have passed since publication of this report but, unfortunately, the United States is still ill-equipped to win the battle of ideas, especially given the existence of important Muslim and pan-Arab broadcasting networks. Perhaps most influential in the continued deterioration of Arab perceptions of the United States is the pan-Arab satellite broadcasting network, *al-Jazeera*. Since its creation in 1996, *al-Jazeera* has become the CNN of the Arab world, reaching some 35 million viewers.

To counter this vast outlet of anti-American sentiment, the United States funded the creation of the Arabic-language *Radio Sawa*. Operated by the International Board of Broadcasters, *Radio Sawa* has established a reputation in the Middle East for reaching out to the Muslim world by devoting the majority of its broadcasting content to Arabic and Western pop music, focusing on listeners below the age of 30. In contrast to the British Broadcasting Corporation (BBC),

Radio Sawa devotes little attention to news programming. *Radio Sawa's* popularity among Arab youth been relatively successful. Unfortunately, by targeting these audiences, *Radio Sawa* has been sowing the seeds for America's loss of the Arab hearts and minds.

Although *Radio Sawa* retains some popularity among young, educated, professional Arabs, this audience, although demographically quite large, has little decision-making impact on the "Muslim street." *Radio Sawa's* hip-hop broadcasts do not reach the real powerbrokers in the tribal societies of the Middle East, the tribal leaders. Throughout the Arab world, tribal leaders act as decision makers and the informal community of these leaders has a decisive impact on the values and behaviors of the youth that compose the "Muslim street."

In order to understand this impact we have to take into consideration the mindset of Wahhabi warriors. First of all, it is crucial to be aware of the extent to which the soldiers of terrorist armies are in fact a by-product of traditional Muslim societies and particularly their rural areas. These rural areas are a repository of Islamic traditions that, over many centuries, have been the foundation of a stable and largely unchanging way of life. It is difficult for citizens of this world to fully escape these traditions and influences, even after they have left their villages and migrated to urban areas or gone abroad.

To understand this phenomenon more fully, let us examine the way of life in traditional Arab villages as it has been described in an Egyptian sociological field study.[192]

In the typical village, Muslim traditions protected the peasants' established way of life from the forcible interference of government bureaucrats. Local authority in these villages depended on the supremacy of Islamic law—the Shari'ah. Order was maintained in peasant society by a traditional administration, which neither the country's government nor the previous colonial administration dared violate. The village administration was comprised of the village elder, his deputies, the commander of the guard, and the Islamic sheikh.

The village elder was the link between the village community and the central authorities. He was chosen from among respected peasant families having extensive ties in the village, and was formally confirmed in his position by the central authorities. As a rule, the post of elder was hereditary, a tradition that the central authorities tended not to disturb so long as tax collection and army recruitment were carried out properly, and civic order was maintained.

The Islamic sheikh, meanwhile, served as the village's religious and moral-legal authority. As the watchdog of fundamentalist traditions and values, he was also the only check on the elder's power. The Islamic sheikh is not appointed formally. He serves independently of the central authorities and is primarily responsible for leading the mosque services.

The Shari'ah admits of no division between spiritual and secular authority, however, and the Islamic sheikh is empowered to bless the authority of the village elder and to consecrate his powers. The sheikh is also empowered to issue an edict discrediting the elder in the event that he publicly offends the sheikh, if he is tyrannical, or if he permits his private army to harass the population. The issuance of an anathema compels the central authorities to remove an elder from his position. The power of the sheikh derives primarily from this protective function. The sheikh is obeyed, feared, respected and loved by all members of the local Muslim community. His opinion can not be challenged by members of the community or outsiders.

Thus, every child reared in a traditional Muslim society must obey two figures outside of his or her family: the administrative boss, or village elder, and the religious leader, or sheikh. The sheikh controls the elder and therefore has the greater authority. It is important to note, however, that in traditional Muslim societies the authority of the sheikh and elder—and the respect that they enjoy from the community at large—come with obligations. A person born into a traditional society is accustomed to obeying these two traditional authority figures, but in return that person expects these leaders to demonstrate concern for his or her private matters and to offer help and aid in time of distress.

In more recent times, mass migration from rural to urban areas has compelled millions of Muslims to break with the traditional ways of life found in isolated villages. In moving to a city, the peasant reared on traditional beliefs discovers that he or she has lost the support of both the village community and its authority figures. Many transplanted peasants also have good memories of their past lives. Not surprisingly, under these circumstances, the newly urbanized peasants typically seek surrogates to replace their traditional support system. Instinctively, they are prepared to follow anyone in their new urban environment—or, for immigrants, in their new country—who helps them to get established in their new life.

Upon arriving in a city, a peasant will typically look for relatives, acquaintances or former neighbors from his or her home village. This penchant for seeking familiar faces, that is, people from home who have established themselves in the new environment, often leads former peasants in Muslim cities to establish fraternal-type organizations or associations. These new urban communities, moreover, tend to replicate the village communities. That is, they have similar political or administrative structures, always headed, as in traditional Muslim villages, by an administrative and a religious leader.

The administrative leader, in this case, may be a person—such as an attorney, a notary, or a wealthy businessman—who holds no official position of authority. But he functions to some extent as a village elder would, by helping newly arrived peasants solve everyday problems, such as dealing with government officials or finding employment and housing. In other words, the administrative leader of a particular community of peasants helps recently arrived members to get established in a new urban environment. One difference between this relationship and the one that exists in the village between peasants and the elder is that, in the city, the administrative leader may demand a fee for his help, or require the peasant to repay him with a service of some sort.

As for the religious leader of an urban-based peasant community, he is likely to be the head of a local mosque, and oversees the religious and moral behavior of the community's various members—including that of the administrative leader. The religious leader is also the primary authority in resolving any inter-family or intra-community problems that might arise for Muslims in the community. As such, and on the basis of Islamic dogmas or rules, the religious leader may demand that specific actions be taken—or avoided—by individual community members. It is important also to remember that members of an urban Muslim community expect to get help from—and give help to—other members of the community. They do not merely work through the administrative and religious leaders. Muslim morality encourages the mutual exchange of services.

Muslims living in urban areas are therefore highly dependent on these informal communities, particularly as they first become accustomed to city life. As time passes, these ties to the community may weaken. But urban Muslims never become entirely independent either of the community's informal rules or, especially, of the authority wielded by its religious leader. And their sheikh's opinions about family life, business affairs, job hunting, and internal or external politics will always influence the members of local Muslim communities.

This same pattern of relationships is replicated to some degree for Muslims who have migrated to the West. One difference, however, is that Muslim communities in the West are typically comprised of immigrants from a particular country rather than from a particular rural area. Thus, each Yemeni, Iraqi, Egyptian or Afghan community in the West also has its own informal administrative and religious leaders. And they play the same general roles as their counterparts in urban communities in the Muslim world. They, too, help recent arrivals to adjust to a new life by providing advice on employment and housing, granting cash loans, recommending immigration lawyers, dealing with local government officials, and facilitating contacts between new arrivals and already established members of the community. These informal community leaders, it is important to note, typically know a great deal about the private problems of various community members. In helping them resolve their problems, the leaders are fully entitled to demand services in return. And, by all means, these informal Muslim community leaders in Western countries are the most important personalities, who have the greatest impact on opinions and behavior of Muslims who have migrated to the West.

This brings us back to the issue of *Radio Sawa*'s broadcasting and its influence on the "Muslim street." Even if *Sawa* managed to win the hearts and minds of some young Arabs and to expand its 15-29 year-old audience by providing them with "accurate, fact-based news and information," this counts for little because broadcasting to such audiences misses the most important informal administrative and religious leaders of Muslim communities in Islamic and Western countries. If the United States hopes to be successful in swaying public opinion on the "Muslim street," it must target Muslim opinion leaders. For these listeners, it is not a matter of listening briefly to a short news synopsis while in a car traveling to an office or home. American radio program directors should understand that Muslim elder listeners have a lot of time for listening to radio and television broadcasting. Based upon my 22 years of experience of dealing with Muslim audiences, I have reached the conclusion that such audiences are prepared to sit in local coffee houses and listen to extended programs for hours or more in order learn about a topic. This is the average length of political programs for Muslim television. Unlike on American programs, the Muslim street prefers that programming on political, economic or theological topics not be interrupted by commercial advertisements or music. It is common in the Muslim broadcasting world for talk show hosts and television program participants to talk for a long time while the program's hosts do not interrupt them. American program directors are also advised to know the history and culture of their particular target audience, where the ideas of tolerant Islam are being spread, as well as the "history of Islam, including the degree to which Islam has spread in a country that is a target for broadcasting."[193] Concentrating American broadcasting efforts on the presentation of current news may turn out to be largely a waste of time and government money, because even this young audience may get their news from commercial Western satellite radio and television stations, which have become very popular in Muslim countries.

The United States needs to recognize that it is waging a "battle of ideas" against Wahhabis, who are responsible for fueling and disseminating anti-American feelings among the population of Arab countries. Consequently, it is important for American policymakers to understand that the battle of ideas is not an academic discussion and is not a free exchange of information. It is a war, where some principles and rules of a free press do not operate. Every kind of war has its own rules and this war is no different.

One reason America is losing the battle of ideas is that U.S. policymakers are applying peacetime rules while their ideological enemies are ignoring these rules. America won the battle of ideas with Communism because it obtained the sympathy of the peoples of the Soviet Union—the "Soviet street." Unfortunately, the United States is seeking to apply its Cold War experience and many of the same techniques in the battle of ideas with Islamists and Baathists. U.S. policymakers should bear in mind that the "Muslim street" differs significantly from the "Soviet street" and America's former experience offers American policymakers little or no help in dealing with the situation in which it currently finds itself in Iraq and the Arab world at large.

Those who are responsible for planning the "battle of ideas" against Wahhabism should take into consideration that the idea of "false Muslims" has been seeded very deeply in the minds of the "Muslim street" and has a major impact on the mentality of ordinary Muslims. That is why Cold War's practice of using "native speakers" to articulate American ideas is not as clever as it may seem. Native speakers will not be perceived in places like Iraq as heroes—like Soviet dissidents were who broadcasted from Voice of America or Radio Free Europe/ Radio Liberty—but as "false Muslims," traitors and collaborators. The American agenda should be articulated by native-born Americans who could deliver their message speaking Arabic with a foreign accent or with the help of simultaneous translators. This is especially important when a message is being delivered in a visual form (television, DVD or VCR tape). Native speakers should be used primarily for delivering news and in discussions about theological problems of Islam because having native Americans participate in discussing the issues of Muslim theology would be highly counterproductive. According to Imam Muslim Hajji of the Bishkek Islamic University in Kyrgyzstan, "[i]f a broadcaster speaks about Islam with a heavy foreign accent, Muslim listeners will consider the content of the program to be something alien, artificially imposed, and not applicable to them... It is desirable to involve highly intellectual, authoritative religious figures who are accepted by the Muslim community of a particular country, region or city. Only well-educated *alim*s (experts on Islam) should comment on and interpret the Holy Qur'an."[194]

The United States should also consider adopting the policy of disseminating free audiocassettes, DVDs and VCR tapes to Muslim audiences, instead of relying solely on *Radio Sawa*. It should also consider providing ordinary Arab listeners with inexpensive radios that can only be tuned to -American radio stations.

If such steps were taken, then America might begin to regain the information advantage in the Muslim world, winning over the important tribal elders residing in the rural regions of the Middle East—an area, it should be noted, where *Radio Sawa* does reach. In places like Iraq, this strategy might play a critical role in bringing community leaders to the side of the United States, thereby turning the tide in this important front in the War on Terror.

OVERCOMING THE LEGACY OF ANTI-SOVIETISM

Only by recognizing the significant differences between today's "Muslim street" and yesterday's "Soviet street" can a winning strategy be forged that will overcome the efforts by *al-Jazeera* and similar outlets to cast the United States as the enemy of Islam.

Most fundamentally, Soviet and Wahhabi propagandists differ in the way they criticize the West. The core message of Soviet propaganda was: "Our life is good and Western life is bad. We are happy and do not need the West." The Soviet leaders erected the Iron Curtain in order to prevent the Soviet people from discovering the positive aspects of Western life. Communist leaders had little difficulty in carrying out this agenda, as the few foreigners who lived within the Soviet Union did so under strict KGB surveillance, which was aimed at blocking contact between them and ordinary Soviet people.

After the Second World War, the United States created the Voice of America and Radio Free Europe/Radio Liberty, which worked with the BBC and West Germany's Deutche Welle to provide the Soviet people with information about Western life; giving them the opportunity to see the better standard of life available in the West. In spite of all the efforts of Soviet propagandists, people living in the USSR and the Soviet bloc began to believe that what came from America was good. Even the word "American" became a synonym for "perfect" in the slang of Soviet youth. And, conversely, the "Soviet street" rejected ideas, policies and concepts issuing from the Communist leadership. Those living behind the Iron Curtain admired pro-Western dissidents and regarded as heroes those Soviet defectors who fought their way through prison and repression to reach the West. The United States was wildly successful in achieving its goal of establishing a positive connotation for itself in the heart and mind of the ordinary Soviet person.

ADAPTING TO THE ARAB MINDSET

Unlike the Soviet bloc, Muslim countries have a considerable American and Western presence through military and civilian projects which have a visible role for local people. No Iron Curtain separates Muslims from the outside world. Ordinary Muslims have had the chance to learn that life in the United States and other Western countries is better than in their own, and realizing this discrepancy, they blame their Muslim governments. Thus, Wahhabi leaders are often placed in a situation where they need to some up with a convincing answer to the question, "Why is my life so much worse than the life of the ordinary Westerner?" Local Wahhabis cannot claim, as their Soviet counterparts did, "Our life is good, and Western life is bad." Instead the Wahhabis answer, "Your life is bad precisely because the life of Westerners is so good." An essential element of U.S. broadcasts and public policy, therefore, must provide an aggressive refutation of this claim.

In attempting to link the "good" and the "positive" with the United States in the heart and mind of the "Muslim street," policymakers must adapt their strategy to suit the current situation. Accurate, fact-based news and information allowed ordinary Soviet citizens to see through the phony rhetoric of "the good Communist life" propagated by the Soviet Union and East bloc governments. However, regardless of the success of the Western norm of balanced news media during the Cold War, this approach damages Western credibility among Arab audiences. As the "Muslim street" perceives it, when Americans address their deficiencies openly, or criticize their president, politicians or army commanders, this is interpreted as weakness. In the eyes of the Muslim audience, this makes the United States look pathetic. To cite one example, during the Iraq war, the U.S. Congress sponsored the creation of *Radio Free Iraq* (RFI). RFI, in turn, broadcast Democratic Party criticism of President Bush and, by doing so, inadvertently strengthened the anti-American claims made by *al-Jazeera*. The United States cannot abandon its balanced presentation of American life without betraying its core principles, but it needs to recognize that such an approach is not a natural winning strategy, as it was during the Cold War. Instead, it is a substantial handicap in the current "battle of ideas." To help overcome this handicap, and in order to stand a chance of prevailing in the battle of ideas against Wahhabism, the United States needs to make much greater efforts to strongly defend American images, ideas and values. It will not be safe for the United States to revert to its natural, peace-time principle of "balanced information" until peace comes to the region.

RECOMMENDATIONS OF CENTRAL ASIAN JOURNALISTS

Central Asian journalists are waging an uncompromising war against Wahhabism in their newspapers, magazines, radio and television broadcasting. American journalists may find such unique experience to be informative in their work.

While dealing with Muslim audiences, Central Asian journalists try to better "understand the target audience of the programs, including understanding the level of their religious awareness and general education." They believe that broadcasting to Muslim audiences "should be a podium for respectable religious figures, who will urge their communities to fight against violence, cruelty and terror."[195] Here are some recommendations about topics for broadcasting programs and print products, from Central Asian experts at fighting Wahhabism ideology in their countries:

- The main idea of monotheism, as stated in the Qur'an and Sunnah of the Prophet Muhammad;
- A critique of the Wahhabi definition of who is unfaithful and who is a true Muslim;
- An examination of who benefits from extremist ideas—groups interested in creating political instability in different countries and in the world in general and those who wish to make a fortune from interethnic conflicts and spreading hatred;
- Islam is religion of peace. An explanation of the instructions of Allah on the necessity of peaceful cooperation between Muslims and other nations, a search for the settlement of emerging conflicts, and the organization of inter-religious and interethnic dialogue;
- Tolerant Islam is the true Islam, which forbids any type of egotism, chaos or despotism. Every man has to make his own choice himself in favor of Islam without pressure. Muhammad forbade violence in attempting to spread the ideas of Islam;
- Understanding *jihad* as a call for all Muslims to display unlimited tolerance and to fight against self weaknesses for the sake of spiritual self-perfection;
- All people are children of Adam and Eve and have equal rights and obligations. Islam draws no distinction among people of different nationalities, languages, and skin colors. The history of Islam demonstrates its commitment to cooperation among Arabs, Ethiopians, Berbers, Persians, Jews and others, within the framework of Islam;
- Mutual understanding and love as key issues in Islam. The Qur'an forbids murder. Thus, a murderer encroaches on a holy right, life, which has been given to people by the Creator;

- The right of non-Muslims or foreigners who live in Muslim countries to have their lives and property protected. Encroachment on their lives and property is forbidden in Islam. Muslim jurisprudence on the "Ahd al-aman," or the obligation to guaranty security for those who visit a Muslim country;

- Respect toward the traditions, customs, cultural and religious peculiarities of different nations as a main characteristic of Islam. It is generally recognized that there is much in common in the doctrines of different religions, especially in their moral values and ideas of life, and in teachings about the aim and meaning of people's existence on Earth. Broadcasters are urged to educate television and radio audiences about mutual respect, and tolerance toward the particularities of other religions;

- The history of good neighborly relations between Muslims and the people of the Book (ahl al-Kitab), i.e., Jews and Christians. The common features in the teachings of Muslims, Christians and Jews. The unity of the people of the Book and Muslims on issues of morality: how the people of the Book and Muslims profess the same virtues granted by the almighty Creator: honor, fidelity, brotherhood, modesty, self-sacrifice, sincerity, mercy, devoted love to one's neighbor, and so on;

- The history of the land of Palestine and Jerusalem, where for more than 1,400 years Muslims, Christians and Jews lived in peace, largely without conflict and war; enjoying the benefits of stability and toleration;

- "All Muslims are brothers by faith; all mankind are brothers by creation" (a statement by the rightful caliph Ali, nephew and son-in-law of Muhammad). All people are creations of Allah, i.e., they are brothers by creation. The main idea of Islam, as well as of other divine religions, is encapsulated in three words (revelations of God): faith, love and toleration;

- "There is no compulsion in religion" (Qur'an, 2:256). The path to faith lies via the heart and mind of every man. The Holy Qur'an and Sunnah do not call Muslims to fight against adherents of other religions in order to convert them to Islam;

- Religious tolerance. The spiritual and physical diversity of mankind is an idea of God, and only Allah can solve divisions among people on the issue of religion;

- No coexistence between Islam and terror. The moral commandments of Islam are against all forms of violence and cruelty. Islamic injunctions against suicide;
- Islam's opposition to violations of human rights, even if they are supposedly being done for the sake of the whole society. The rights of an individual must be as respected, as are the rights of all people taken together;
- The immorality of using religion for political or national aims. The only aim of religion is to satisfy a person's spiritual needs. All religions of the world testify to the thirst for God on the part of human beings. Spirituality stems from the wish to grow closer to God; the morality of an individual proceeds from spirituality, and, thus, a tolerant way of life is intended for the entire human community.[196]

CONCLUSION

To win the War on Terror, the United States and its allies must win the battle for the hearts and minds of the "Muslim street." No longer can the West rely on Cold War techniques and the notion of an opponent who is vulnerable to a simple explanation of Western life as it is. Policymakers must understand that for the "Muslim street" the West is perceived as the reason why ordinary Muslims suffer. This misperception and argument by the Wahhabis must be countered using methods appropriate to a time of ideological warfare, including actively promoting the image of a beneficent America. Consideration must be paid to the manner in which an Arab audience receives and filters its information. Most importantly, the proper audience must be identified and aggressively targeted if the United States is to be successful

Unlike during the Cold War, the United States should adopt a policy of reaching out to the Arabs that pursues the following points:

- Emphasize that the United States is not making the lives of Arabs miserable, and do so in an aggressive way without undue concern about the opinions of Arab governments.
- Demonstrate that the United States is providing significant assistance to Muslims and Arabs and that America continues to work hard to

improve the lives of the Iraqi and Arab peoples in an effort to make them happier.

- Demonstrate that American values are not at odds with Islam and that the United States does not wish to force its values or its system upon Muslim countries.
- Stress that America is a peaceful, although a very strong, nation and that willingness to use force in Afghanistan and Iraq stands as a clear warning to those who wish to challenge the United States.
- Adopt some of the more successful information tactics of militant Islam. It would be wise for the United States to disseminate free audiotapes, DVDs and VCR tapes with American messages in local languages to Muslim audiences, as well as provide Muslims with inexpensive radios that can only be tuned to American-friendly stations.
- Expand Arab educational exchange programs with the United States, in order to increase the number of Americans who are proficient in the Arabic language. In addition, use these exchanges as a means to establish contacts with Islamic moderates who might take part in theological discussions designed to challenge proponents of militant Islam and Ba'athism.
- Target tribal elders in Iraq and the Middle East rather than focusing on the teenage youth market favored by *Radio Sawa*. Given that the tribal society of Iraq is ruled by senior tribal leaders, who spend hours each day listening to *al-Jazeera* or other stations, it is necessary for the United States to develop radio programs that target Iraqi elders rather than the youth, due to the elders' influence on decision making in Iraq's hierarchical society.

FIGHTING WAHHABISM IN EDUCATIONAL ESTABLISHMENTS

Central Asian educators clearly understand the importance and their responsibility for protecting the young generation of their countries from being corrupted by Wahhabi ideology. They do not want to follow the schemas for general and religious education that have been forced upon schools and universities in various Muslim countries by Wahhabis and their Saudi sponsors. The most striking examples of such wrong-headed educational systems were in Afghanistan under the Taliban, in Algeria, in the Chechen Republic and other countries where the Wahhabis are powerful. According to Imam Muslim Hajji of Kyrgyzstan's Bishkek Islamic University:

> People who call themselves "correct Muslims" have distorted the regulations of Islam and have changed the content of a Muslim education. In order to correct this situation, one needs to have a true and good education. It is necessary to teach the youth what is right and what is wrong; what leads to the good, and what evokes evil. Everything that one needs in life should be taught in schools, and colleges. This kind of information includes knowledge about a healthy life, good neighborhood, Muslim patience, and, as Prophet Muhammad (PBUH) taught, "Let the one who believes in Allah and the Last Day not cause harm to the neighbor."[197]

Imam Muslim Hajji, who graduated from Egypt's renowned Al-Azhar Islamic University, regrets that:

> ...the amount of books published in the Arab world does not exceed 1.1% of the world total. At the same time, Arabs comprise 5% of the world's population. The number of religious books comprises 17% of the total amount of books issued in Arab countries, whereas in other countries it is only 5% of the book market. In Arab countries, there is a lack of effective systems to promote knowledge and innovations. There are no reasonable policies directed to strengthening the distribution and development of information. Today, one is considered to be a scholar in Muslim countries depending on what he knows from the Qur'an, how many hadiths he can quote, and how many proverbs and sayings he can cite as arguments in a discussion.[198]

Central Asian governments have taken very important steps to delegitimize the ideology of Wahhabism, to limit its ideological influence on local Muslims, and to inculcate immunity to Wahhabism in the hearts and minds of local youth, in order to prevent them from joining radical Islamist organizations and terrorist groups. Central Asian governments, especially those in Uzbekistan and Kyrgyzstan, have created and developed an educational system—from kindergarten to the university level—that instills the moral norms and social principles of tolerant Islam, and that respects the value of all human life (Muslim, Christian, Jewish, or other). The Central Asian governments rely on the support of local Muslim scholars, who advocate tolerant Islam. Since Wahhabi ideology is at odds with mainstream Islam, such scholars have had their own reasons to speak out against militant Islamists.

While traveling in the Central Asian republics during the summer of 2006, I met a number of educators who proposed writing textbooks and curricula for lessons on ethics and faith, which incorporate the ideas of tolerant Islam, and translating them into English, Arabic, Urdu and other Middle Eastern languages, to be used in schools and *madrassas* in Afghanistan, Iraq and other Muslim countries. I believe that their proposals may be valuable for U.S. authorities who are responsible for the postwar reconstruction of the national educational systems in Afghanistan and Iraq. Otherwise, these educational establishments may be equipped with Wahhabi textbooks. Such actions by American authorities would limit Wahhabi ideological influence and help to innoculate the hearts and minds of youth against Wahhabism—which, in turn, will prevent them from joining radical Islamist organizations and terrorist groups.

Central Asian Islamic educators have devised systems for teaching the principles of tolerant Islam at primary school, secondary school, and university levels. Some important, representative examples of their efforts are outlined in detail below.

THE UNIVERSITY LEVEL

Dr. Zukhriddin Munimovich Khusnidinov, rector of the Islamic University in Tashkent, Uzbekistan, believes that radical Islamists do not understand the essence of Islam. He believes that it is very important to educate youth and give young people a proper understanding of Islamic principles and their implementation in real life. The Tashkent Islamic University challenges Wahhabi ideology and does its best to insert proper Islamic studies into the existing curricula of schools, colleges and universities. The Islamic University supervises working teams that prepare textbooks for educational establishments at all levels. The teams include experts in Islamic law, in state law, in pedagogic sciences, and in sociology as well as representatives of the government. The teams select educational establishments in different regions of the country to test the system before introducing it on the total national level. The Islamic University has its own television studio, where students prepare programs on Islamic issues for local television, and these programs are very popular on state and private channels.[199]

Because the Tashkent Islamic University plays a major role in Central Asian battle of ideas against Wahhabi ideology, it is worth describing its activities in detail.

The Tashkent Islamic University was established in 1999 by a decree of the President of the Republic of Uzbekistan, Islam Karimov. The decree stated that the purpose of the university was:

> preserving the rich spiritual and cultural heritage of the sacred faith of Uzbek people—the religion of Islam; deep and comprehensive study, conducting scientific-theoretical research, analyzing and developing contemporary ideas and scientific research based on the works of great scholars of the Uzbek land; providing the training of qualified specialists in accordance with modern requirements and creating the necessary conditions for them; as well as raising the religious literacy of Uzbek people through the study of unique "Uzbekce" [samples of old Uzbek culture] inherited from Uzbek ancestors.

The university states that it has the following goals:
- training highly qualified specialists who have mastered the religion, history and philosophy of Islam and its role in the life of society and development, who are capable of solving theoretical and practical issues encountered by the state, social institutions and religious organizations;
- upgrading the knowledge of existing specialists;
- studying of the expertise of world-renowned higher educational institutions comprehensively, and organizing the educational system of the Tashkent Islamic University according to modern standards;
- restoring, analyzing and developing the rich religious-scientific and theoretical heritage of the Uzbek people's ancestors;

- reviewing the results of research and disseminating them to the general public;
- defining the role and importance of Islam on the basis of research into the place of Islam in world history;
- researching Islam's ideas, norms and trends in its theoretical and practical development;
- writing and publishing manuals, teaching materials and textbooks on religion, in particular on the study and philosophy of Islam;
- developing a mutually beneficial cooperative relationship with leading international educational and scientific centers;
- producing harmoniously developed and devoted individuals, dedicated to respect for national and human values, national traditions, and the spirit of religious tolerance.

The Islamic University conducts research in the following fields:

The Qur'an and its interpretation
The university has many manuscripts about the Qur'an and interpretations of it. Studying them should clear up facts belonging to different periods in Islamic history.

Hadiths
The university has a great variety of manuscripts of hadiths and commentaries on them. The task is to study them, and to summarize the results and make them available to the general public.

Fikh—the science of Islamic law
The work *Al-Hidayah* by the famous Islamic scholar and jurist Burhan al-Din al-Marghinani is usually taken as the basis of Islamic jurisprudence in Central Asia, as well as Turkey and the Indian subcontinent. The university has many research studies, treatises, manuscripts and commentaries on it.

Uzbek history, and the lives and activities of famous religious leaders and their works

The different Islamic establishments that existed until the 13ᵗʰ Century: documents concerning mosques, educational institutions, permissions, waqf certificates, correspondence and decisions, and documents on religious establishments

The history of Islam as related in the works of the many travelers who visited Central Asia beginning in the 9ᵗʰ and 10ᵗʰ centuries AD

The university has the writings of Istakhriy, Khurdadbek, Ibn Batuta, Makhodusy, Yokhut Khamaviy, Lui Ganzales de Klavikho, Ibn Arabshokh and other travelers, and also Russian officers who visited this region in later centuries.

The works of poets and writers, folklore, memorials on Islamic culture and "Uzbekces"

I have visited the university many times and noted that the land and buildings of the university are furnished in accordance with modern requirements. There are modern amenities for students to study and relax. Well-lighted and spacious classrooms are equipped with up-to-date equipment, including computers. There are special language laboratories and Internet terminals. There is also a sizable library.

The faculty follows Islamic educational traditions, which have existed for more than a thousand years, and also study the experience of the most advanced and well known foreign universities and scientific-research centers in United States, the United Kingdom, France, Egypt, the United Arab Emirates, Saudi Arabia, Kuwait and other countries.

The following departments of the university are in charge of training and research for undergraduate students, post-graduate students and faculty.

RELIGIOUS AND ISLAMIC STUDIES DEPARTMENT

The Religious and Islamic Studies Department is one of the leading departments of the university. It seeks to:

- educate highly skilled specialists who possess a comprehensive knowledge of the principles of Islam, understand the role of religion in society, know the history of Islam and understand secular sciences, and are able to

solve the theoretical and practical problems of public, state and religious institutions;
- prepare lecturers on Islamic issues;
- draw upon the rich religious, scientific, and theoretical heritage of the Uzbek ancestors, comprehensively studying, analyzing, researching, translating and publish historically-based studies;
- be engaged in scientific works in Islamic studies, especially Islamic teachings, in composing textbooks and manuals on religious studies for continuing education and public use;
- train highly skilled religious experts in Islam.

The staff of the department teaches the following courses:
- Religious Studies,
- Islamic Studies,
- Islamic "Uzbekce,"
- History and Philosophy of Islam,
- Hadith and Hadith Studies,
- Qur'an and *Tafsir*,
- Interpretation of the Qur'an,
- Theology of Islam,
- Principles of Islam,
- Oratory Skills,
- Methodology of Teaching Religious Topics,
- Practical Training on Foreign Special Literature,
- Uzbek Classic Literature.

Research activities of the department
The lecturers of the department are researching topics such as:
- "The role of the scholars of Mavaraunnakhr and Hurasan in developing the science of hadith,"
- "The importance of the verses and *tafsir*s of the Qur'an and hadiths in the fight against religious fundamentalism,"
- "The development of hadith science in Samarkand (8-12th centuries),"
- "The role of the Sunnah in the formation of Hanafi Islam,"
- "Research on Bahrul Ilm's work on Abu Lays Samarkandi,"
- "Ethical issues in Maqomat's work on Zamahshariy,"

- "The experience of England in religion (a field study of religious organizations),"
- "The history of trends in Islam."

This department has established cooperative relations with universities in Egypt, Kuwait, Saudi Arabia, Japan, Turkey, Iran, and France. It organizes scientific seminars, conferences and roundtable discussions in conjunction with the Tashkent State Institute of Oriental Studies, the Abu Rayhon Beruniy Oriental Studies Institute, the Tashkent Cultural Center of Egypt, the National University of Uzbekistan, the Committee of Religious Affairs under the Cabinet of Ministers of the Republic of Uzbekistan, the Imam Bukhari Scientific-Enlightenment Center and Tashkent Islamic Institute.

THE DEPARTMENT OF ISLAMIC LAW

The main goal of this department is to teach *Fiqh* or Islamic law, together with the secular law courses on the basis of scientific works that were inherited from national experts in Islamic law.

The following courses are offered by the department:
- "Usulul *Fiqh*"—the principles and methodologies of Islamic law
- "Fur'ul *fiqh*"—the different fields of Islamic law
- Legal systems of Muslim countries
- Modern legal sciences
- Directions in Islam and specific ideas of the Hanafi school
- The legal works of Central Asian experts in Islamic law, according to modern standards.

The research activities of the department
The department conducts research on 28 different areas of "Islamic Law." Since the 2003-2004 academic year, courses in "Islamic law" and "Legal systems of Muslim countries" have been introduced for the master's degree students.

The department's faculty and students conduct research in following fields:
- Islamic law
- The participation of Central Asian experts in developing Islamic law
- The comparative study of Islamic law with other legal systems
- The methodology of Islamic law

- *Fiqh* science and the place of Movaraunnakhr scholars in its development.

The department's faculty has written the following monographs and books:
- *Religious Fundamentalism and its Threat to the Security of a Society*
- *Islamic Law, the Hanafi School and Central Asian Islamic Law Experts*
- *Sufi Spiritual Principles and Human Beings*
- *Marghinani and his Followers*
- *East and Human Rights*
- *Constitutional Rights in the Republic of Uzbekistan*
- *Constitutions of Foreign Countries*
- *International Law*
- *Standards of Humanity*
- *The World of Constitutions*
- *Criminal and Legal Problems in the Fight against Religious Fundamentalism and Terrorism*
- *Tax Legacy and Financial Law*
- *The Role of Education of Law in Forming Legal Awareness.*

THE DEPARTMENT OF INTERNATIONAL ECONOMIC RELATIONS

This department educates highly skilled economists who can speak two foreign languages (Arabic and a Western language) and have knowledge in the fields of international economic relations (bachelor's) and the economy of foreign countries (master's).

Research activities of the department
This department offers courses, seminars and practical trainings on topics such as: international economic relations, international foreign exchange and credit relations, international marketing, international trade and business, international diplomatic relations, international management, the world economy, the economy of Islamic countries, principles of Islamic economy, foreign economic activity, international economic integration, trade and business in Islam, Islamic countries in the world economy, international economic statistics, social security in Islam, finance and banking in Islam and international financial relations.

The professors and lecturers of the department carry out research on the modern market economy, trade and business in Islam, the economy of Islamic countries, *zakat*, charity, social security in Islam, *waqf*, the interest-free banking system in Islam, and other related topics.

The lecturers of the department teach the following courses:
- Qur'anic verses related to the economy
- establishing and managing small and medium size enterprises
- methods of finance in the international economy
- comparative study of business relations in Islam
- young economist
- property relations in a free economy
- English for business
- business administration.

THE COMPUTER AND NATURAL SCIENCES DEPARTMENT

The main tasks of this department are facilitating information exchange, accelerating the use of new pedagogic methods (online conversations and teacher-student exchanges) at all lectures in the university, organizing "open lectures" and "problem lectures" for every department, and providing facilitating research work.

Research activities of the department
The staff of this department have developed the university's Web site and produced e-books such as: *Interpretation of the meanings of the Holy Qur'an, Hadiths, The Relationship between the Holy Qur'an and Natural Sciences*, and *An Electronic Tour of the Historical Monuments of Bukhara*.

THE DEPARTMENT OF ORIENTAL STUDIES

This department teaches Arabic, Persian and Uzbek languages, as well as oriental "Uzbekces" and the translations of them.

THE DEPARTMENT OF WESTERN LANGUAGES

This department teaches English, French, German and Russian languages in all colleges of the university.

THE DEPARTMENT OF PHILOSOPHY

The goals of the Philosophy Department are to:
- provide undergraduate and postgraduate students with a fundamental knowledge of philosophy, the philosophy of religion, and the philosophy of Islam;
- familiarize students with the spiritual heritage of national ancestors who considerably contributed to world philosophy, religion and Islam.
- create a wide scope of popular scientific works, textbooks and educational-methodological manuals.

The faculty of this department lecture on: the fundamentals of philosophy, the idea of national independence, Sufism, logic, the philosophy of religion, the psychology of religion, the sociology of religion, and the philosophy of Islam.

THE ISLAMIC RESEARCH CENTER

The center conducts research activities aimed at:
- defining the role and importance of Islam in the current multi-religious environment, in the world, in Central Asia and in Uzbekistan, on the basis of studying the place of Islam in the history of world civilization;
- creating and publishing popular works, textbooks, training programs and material on theology, in particular on the philosophy of Islam;
- cooperating with the leading training and scientific centers of foreign countries.

The center has chairs in the following areas: the studying of the Qur'an and *tafsir*, hadith studies, the history and philosophy of Islam, *fiqh*, depository studies and manuscript studies.

The center's research includes studies on:
- Studying the Qur'an and *tafsir*;
- *Fiqh* science and the place of Movaraunnakhr scholars in its development;
- Determining, analyzing and publishing the sources of the history, philosophy, enlightenment and values of Islam;
- The methodology of Islamic law;

- Scientific and theoretical principles of establishing an encyclopedic dictionary of terms and idioms on the basis of Islamic sources.

The center had published such books as *Pearls of Ethics, Uzbek Great Ancestors* (in English, Arabic and Uzbek), and *The Holy Qur'an on the Prophet Jesus.*

THE CULTURAL HERITAGE DEPOSITORY

The Cultural Heritage Depository gathers works representing the religious heritage created by Uzbek ancestors, restores them, and passes them down to future generations for research, publishing and cataloging. There are 192 manuscripts and 655 ancient scripts and 1311 modern books in the depository. Intensive work is being done to restore, categorize and create catalogues. The 1311 modern books were gifts from Egypt, Saudi Arabia, Jordan and Kuwait. There is a special commission for evaluating and accepting manuscripts from the public. A commission determines the name and date of publication and scientific importance of the books that are collected from the public in order to evaluate them. After evaluation, the university purchases manuscripts from the public.

The number of books in the depository is continually increasing. There are books about *tafsirs*, hadith, Islamic law and the history of Islam, which are published in Arab or Islamic countries.

THE SCIENTIFIC SOCIETY OF STUDENTS

The Scientific Society of Students of the University was established in order to support talented youth, and to:
- provide and develop scientific opportunities for students;
- direct intellectual potential of the students towards scientific researches;
- invite students to write dissertation thesis and fulfill scientific research;
- help publishing articles of talented students;
- help talented students to participate in different conferences and seminars.

Students who have begun scientific work are assigned highly-ranked professors as their supervisors. These supervisors help students to choose actual topics and research on the chosen topic. The Head of the Society will then give recommendations to financially support students who are doing excellent scientific research. The Society's annual scientific meeting takes place every academic year during April-May. Students from all departments participate in the meeting and make reports on different topics such as "Interpration of the meanings of Holy Qur'an", "Selected Hadiths from Imam al-Buhariys," "Qudsiy Hadiths," and "A thousand Hadith." The Society has plans to develop relations with students of other universities.

The Kamolot Youth Social Movement

The Kamolot youth social movement of Tashkent Islamic University was established in May 2001. The movement states that its aims and functions are to:

- fight against harmful ideologies that are trying to spoil peaceful Uzbek life and to block Uzbek ways, which we chose, and to increase loving and peaceful feelings among the students
- organize students meetings in accordance with the standards of Islamic ethics for a healthy life within the university and with students of other local universities;
- organize the participation of students in the discussions of law projects dedicated to youth and on various sport, cultural, economical and social issues that are related to the problems of youth;
- help the students to gain modern international economic knowledge and to use it in practice;
- organize sport activities in the university.

The University's Scientific-Analytic Bulletin

The university's *Scientific-Analytic Bulletin* publishes research studies by professors and researchers as well as the texts of speeches made during conferences and seminars at Tashkent Islamic University. The bulletin examines:

- the theory of religious studies
- oriental sciences
- the history and "Uzbekces" of Islam
- Islamic law
- Qur'anic studies
- hadith studies
- the philosophy of Islam

- Sufi spiritual principles
- directions in Islam.

During the last 15 years of independence, the Soviet-era atheistic approach towards religion was abandoned and Uzbekistan's approach towards religion and religious people has changed completely. New Uzbek religious studies were established in accordance with the standards of world religious studies. Islamic studies were recognized as a science and much scientific-theoretical research was carried out. As a result, from 2002 to 2004, more than 80 scholarly articles on different topics such as religious studies, the philosophy and history of Islam, *fiqh*, and Sufi spiritual principles have been published.

THE *ISLAM ZIYOSI* (LIGHT OF ISLAM) NEWSPAPER

The students of Tashkent Islamic University began publishing their *Islam Ziyosi* newsletter in December 2003. The newsletter is published twice a month. The newsletter states that its main tasks are:
- Studying, analyzing and developing both the rich religious and secular heritage of Uzbek ancestors;
- To demonstrate the role and importance of Islam in the Uzbek republic and the world in the current situation of religious tolerance, by studying the role of Islam in world civilization;
- Publishing information about the philosophy, history and teachings of Islam; informing youth about the works of great Uzbek ancestors;
- Publishing translations and the originals of manuscripts on Qur'anic, hadith and Islamic law studies;
- To spread classical views of Islam and religious tolerance among youth.

STUDIO ZIYO

The production company Studio Ziyo was established at Tashkent Islamic University and is funded by the university. The studio's main task is to prepare programs and films dedicated to national and religious values and to broadcast them every Friday via the main channel of Uzbek television on a program called "On the way of strengthening the faith." In addition, every Ramadan it broadcasts films under a program called "The Present of Ramadan."

The studio has made 118 programs and 20 films. It also records different events, translates films, advertises films, and provides computer animation, musical clips and video copying.

Since July 2002, the studio has offered Internet provider service at special discounted rates. This service provides a very good opportunity to university students, lecturers and researchers, including Internet connections to personal computers. The main customers are public schools, university students and high school pupils.

THE IMPACT OF TASHKENT ISLAMIC UNIVERSITY'S EFFORTS

In recent years, Uzbekistan has taken practical actions to fight the ideology of Wahhabism and, together with international religious organizations and UNESCO, organized international scientific conferences on "World Religions in Support of the Culture of Peace" (Tashkent, 2000) and "Islam and the Secular Enlightened State" (Samarkand, 2002). A conference on "Religious Tolerance in Uzbekistan and France" was held on March 15, 2004 in Paris. Also, an international scientific conference on "Special Aspects of Religious Tolerance and Extremism in Central Asia" was held at Tashkent Islamic University.

In 2003, the first 97 graduating students of Tashkent Islamic University received their bachelor's degrees. Today, about 100 persons graduate annually from the university, and senior thesis research papers written by them play a significant role in the battle of ideas against Wahhabi ideology. In fact, the students' senior theses form the initial research in this field. In their research, the students consult with original textbooks in Arabic, Persian, English, German, French and Russian.

For example, the senior thesis of J. Takhirov, a student specializing in Religious-Islamic Studies, was devoted to the "Analysis of Approaches in Studying World Religions." In it, Takhirov compared the origins of various world religions. D. Makhsudov's senior thesis on "Abu al-Barakat al-Nasafi and His Role in the Development of *Tafsir* [Qur'anic Interpretation]" provides information about the famous imam, Abu al-Barakat al-Nasafi, who made a great contribution to the development of the Hanafi school of Islamic thought. Makhsudov's senior thesis became a textbook for local high schools. His other book "Madorik at-tanzil va haqoyiq at-ta'wil" (Understanding the Qur'an and the truth of Ta'wil) is used as a textbook on *tafsir* in religious institutions.

The senior thesis of O. Sarsenboyev, a student of Islamic Law, which is titled "The Qur'an and its Legal Classification Norms," studies the basis for three types of criteria for Qur'anic judgments—according to the categories of the Shar'iah, the order of revelation of the Qur'an's verses, and legal aspects. F. Sultanov's senior thesis was devoted to "Issues of the State System in Islam." It elucidates the concept of the state in Islam and its role in Islamic law, reviewing the opinions of scholars in this field.

The university's students specializing in international economic relations researched comparative issues of the economics of Islam. For example, the senior thesis of B. Bobocholov was titled "Issues of Extortion in the Economics of Islam (in the Area of Financial Relations)."

Students specializing in computer and information technology created electronic and multimedia products. For example, A. Marufov created an electronic book of well-known Islamic scholar A. Mansurov's *Interpretation of the Meanings of the Noble Qur'an*. One can use this book to read Uzbek texts of the Qur'an in the Latin, Cyrillic and Arabic alphabets, listen to a recitation of the Qur'an designed for those learning it by heart, and locate Chapters and verses using convenient searching systems. O. Dadamukhammedov's senior thesis was devoted to "An Exhaustive Electronic Book of Hadiths" in which texts of hadiths from the books of *Al-Jome' as-Sahih* by Imam Al-Bukhari, *Sunan at-Termiziy* by Abu Iso Muhammad at-Termiziy, *Tanbehul-g'ofiliyn* by Abul Lays Samarqandiy, *Holy Hadiths* prepared by A. Mansur for publication, and *1001 Hadiths* are gathered in Arabic and Uzbek (in both Latin and Cyrillic alphabets).

Tashkent Islamic University's staff and students believe it necessary to promote religious tolerance as well as national values and traditions in order to create a basis for stability in Uzbek society and to provide for international security and the future of humanity.

It is not an overstatement to say that the activities of Tashkent Islamic University can serve as a model of an Islamic educational institution set up to train experts in tolerant, peaceful Islam. It would be useful to draw upon the experience of the

university's experts to produce curricula and textbooks for schools in Muslim
countries, especially on such delicate subjects as teaching students about theology
in general and Islam in particular.

THE SECONDARY SCHOOL LEVEL

Dr. Akhadjon A. Khasanov, Tashkent Islamic University's professor of history,
has relevant ideas about creating a textbook for teaching the subject "A History of
Religions" at high schools in Muslim countries, as detailed below. Dr. Khasanov
has prepared a table of contents and written several Chapters for such a textbook.
If he receives a serious offer from an interested publisher, he would be able to
complete the textbook. Such a book would be a valuable tool as an alternative
to the Wahhabi textbooks that dominate the classrooms of Islamic *madrassas* all
over the world.

TABLE OF CONTENTS

FOREWORD

In the Introduction, titled "Nations and Religions," students will receive an answer to the question "What is a religion?" Then they will find out about primary religious ideas, the division of religions into national and world religions, and the main differences between them.

In addition, they will have an idea of the place that religions hold in the life of people and the tasks to be fulfilled by religion in a society.

In studying the first part, titled "The Religions of the Ancient World," students will be introduced to what the religious idea is and realize their different forms as totemic, animistic, fetish and other forms.

The other themes of this part will introduce students to polytheistic religions that existed in ancient Egypt, Babylon, Greece and Rome.

In the second part, titled "National Religions of Asian nations," students will be introduced to the history of more than 10 religions, and the similarities and differences among them. He/she will also get to know about the past and present status of Hinduism, Shintoism and Judaism in the life of the Indian, Japanese, and Jewish peoples.

In the third part, titled "The World Religions," students will become acquainted with the history of the emergence of three world religions, their teachings, customs and traditions, and holidays, in accordance with their peculiarities as they developed.

In addition, they will receive information about our great ancestors and their contribution to the development of Islam. The authors have tried to emphasize the educational significance of habits provided by examples from life.

The fourth part of the textbook is titled "Religion and the State." In this Chapter, students will learn the content of the notion "religious fundamentalism," which is often used in the mass media nowadays.

At the same time, students will learn the content of the notions of the "secular state," "religious liberty" and how relations between a state and religion are regulated. In addition, they will learn information about recent changes in attitude towards religion and religious organizations.

Introduction: Nations and Religions

ABOUT A RELIGION
You have heard the word "mosque." At dawn, a muezzin in your *mahalla* (community) says *azon* (the call for morning prayers). You can tell that the morning prayers begin with the words "Allahu akbar, Allahu akbar." Everyday, you see that some people living in your comm nity go to the mosques to pray and some of them pray at home. And you have heard about the word "joynamoz," which is a special piece of cloth on which you pray.

In addition, every Friday most people go to mosques for Friday prayers (juma nomoz). And you know such notions as "Allah," "prophet," "angels," "shaitan [devil]," praying five times daily, "ruza," "hajj" "sacred book," and "hayit." Somebody (your parents or teachers) told you about them.

At the same time, members of your family express such wishes as "Allahga shukur"—"Thank God," "Yaratganga shukur"—"Thanks for the Creator," "Allah hammamizga uzoq umr bersin"—"May God give a long life to all of us," or such requests as "May the deceased be in Paradise and the other people be healthy."

The above mentioned notions, phrases, wishes and request are religious notions. The word "din" is an Arabic word and means "belief" or "faith." It is a belief that Allah created all animate and inanimate things, including human beings, and belief in sacred books and prophets.

NATIONS AND RELIGIONS

There are more than 200 countries in the world in which more than 6 billion people live. They speak in various languages. At the same time, their religions are different. Even in a primitive society, our ancestors had a various religious beliefs—totemism, animis m, fetishism, shamanism and so on. Nowadays, the scholars divide religions into national and world religions.

The national religions are Hinduism, Sikhism, Jainism, Krishnaism, Shintoism, Confucianism and Judaism. These religions are the faith and belief of a number of separate nations. Some religions are spread widely all over the world; they consist of three religions: Buddhism, Christianity and Islam. The world religions are not religions of a separate nation. The representatives of various nations believe in the world religions despite differing nationalities, languages, races and birthplaces.

THE PLACE OF RELIGIONS IN THE LIFE OF PEOPLE AND THE TASKS FULFILLED BY THEM

Religions fulfill special tasks in a society. First, a religion fulfills the task of forming a world outlook. It explains how the world came into existence. It explains the place that human beings hold in the world and the aim of their existence. The religion also fulfills the task of soothing human beings. When a human being has some hardships or troubles, he or she can have found a calming, soothing and reassuring force from religion from time immemorial. When somebody passes away in one's family, the people who come to express condolences to the relatives of the deceased say: "It is the will of Allah. Death is the right thing. May the deceased be in Paradise and the other people be healthy," and in this way they soothe his relatives.

At the same time, religion also plays the part of a unifier. Every religion calls on its followers to obey its rules and demands to be faithful to these rules. So, it unites its followers.

Another task of religion is to regulate and to control the life of the faithful. Religions call on their believers to be in touch with others and to take part in religious customs, traditions and holidays together. So, the religion fulfills the task of getting people in touch with each other.

Over the centuries, religion has helped people to live in cooperation with each other. For thousands of years, it has strengthened the feeling of trust, enabling people to regard the future with hope. It has given people the strength to cope with hardships, difficulties and problems. Religion, which embodies all the moral and ethical qualities cherished by human beings, has spread them for centuries.

Summing up the significance of religion, one can say that religion helps people follow the right trail, be a good person and leave good works after themselves.

ZOROASTRIANISM

THE EMERGENCE OF ZOROASTRIANISM

Zoroastrianism originated in the territory of the ancient Central Asian country of Khorezm. It emerged more than 2700 years ago. The religion was named after its founder and prophet, Zarathustra or Zartosht, who scholars believe lived in about 1000 BC.

In Europe, Zarathustra was known by the name Zoroastr (golden star). The Greeks cherished Zarathustra as a scholar and expert on celestial bodies—an astrologer thinker.

What made Zarathustra create a new religion? Before Zorastriansm, every tribe had its own religion. This was an obstacles to the development of society and prevented the tribes from uniting, which encouraged intertribal war.

In addition, it was advantageous to create a strong, united state to resist attacks from invaders. But the different religions of tribes caused them to live separately from other tribes. A new religion was necessary to create a united State. Great Zarathustra understood this.

As was written in the sacred book, on one of the days of Navruz [the spring equinox], Zarathustra followed the magic ray and met the great god Ahura Mazda. The god Ahura Mazda announced to Zarathustra that he was his prophet. Zarathustra was given the task of telling people that the universe had been created by the God Ahura Mazda. At that time, Zarathustra was 40 years old. In this way, Zarathustra became the prophet of the new religion—Zoroastrianism.

THE SACRED BOOK OF ZOROASTRIANISM

The sacred book of Zoroastrianism is the Avesta. As stated in the "Avesta," its text was sent to Zarathustra by angels.

During the period of Alexander the Great of Macedonia, three-fifths of the Avesta was destroyed. Only its sections on astronomy, philosophy and medicine were translated into the Greek language. The Zoroastrian clergy were killed.

In the third Century AD, the Persian ruler Ardashir restored the existing parts of the Avesta. In the next Century, during the reign of the Persian Sassanid king Shapur, the Avesta was written down as a separate book.

During the rule of the Arabs, the Avesta was banned. Some Persian Zoroastrian believers who did not want to become Muslims escaped to India. Their descendants now live in the city of Mumbai and the state of Gujarat and still profess the Zoroastrian faith. Some Zoroastrian believers live in Persia and other countries.

ABOUT AHURA MAZDA

Zoroastrianism teaches that Ahura Mazda is the only god. Ahura Mazda created all the creatures, things and celestial bodies on Earth and in the heavens. According to the teaching of Zoroastrianism, Ahura Mazda is alive forever. It is the defender of all good deeds, good morals and justice on Earth. At the same time, Ahura Mazda is the enemy of all bad deeds and evil. It fights for the victory of justice. But Ahura Mazda is not alone in the fight for justice. Six angels help it. The angels are also eternal. Ahura Mazda lives behind the Sun.

ZOROASTRIANISM ON THE FIGHT FOR KINDNESS AND AGAINST EVIL

Zoroastrianism teaches that the world is built on kindness and evil. These two forces are always on the process of fighting against each other. Ahura Mazda is the defender of life, kindness, light, justice and all other good things.

The evil spirit Ahr*Iman* sends evil, injustice and darkness into the world. It is the cause of all evil. Ahura Mazda causes kindness. Ahr*Iman* fights against Ahura Mazda and leads people away from the right path.

One day, kindness will win over evil. But for to happen, this people should be truthful and consistent in their words, and officials should be humane. These features of the religion teach people to differentiate kindness from evil. The people who strive for kindness follow the laws, advice and admonitions sent by Ahura Mazda.

THE FORMATION OF THE WORLD IN THE TEACHING OF ZOROASTRIANISM

The book of Zoroastrianism says that the world will exist for 12,000 years. This history consists of four periods, each of which is 3,000 years long. During the first period, there was nothing. During the second period, Ahura Mazda created the heavens, stars, the moon, the sun the first human being and the first animal. The first man and woman gave birth to children. During the third period, the world was flooded, causing the danger of the disappearance of plants, animals and human beings. At this time, the prophet Yima was a great help to them.

Ahura Mazda informed Yima about the forthcoming storm. Yima built a special house and selected pairs of animals from the best breeds. He did the same with the plants. But Yima ate the beef, which had been forbidden by Ahura Mazda. As a result, he was punished by God. Because of this, human beings became mortal.

In the life of mankind, a fight began to return the world back to its original form—eternal kindness. What must be done to return the world to eternal kindness? For this it is necessary to live honestly, to work honestly, to banish evil from the human heart, to help orphans and poor people, to have good intentions, tell the truth and say good words.

At the end of the fourth period, goodness will triumph over evil. Evil and death will be defeated. All dead people will return to life. All sinful people will be sorry for their transgressions and will not commit any more sins because evil no longer exists. A period of peace and prosperity will begin throughout the world. There will be no evil, envy, meanness or duplicity.

THE FOUR SACRED ELEMENTS

In Zoroastrianism, fire, earth, water and air are considered to be the four sacred elements. Fire is the symbol of the god Ahura Mazda. It was especially cherished in Zoroastrian temples. Before making a fire, a clergyman would put on a white robe and a white cap on his head. His face was covered by a white cover, which prevented the sacred fire from being polluted by human breath.

Zoroastrianism also teaches that sowing seeds of plants puts an end to evil. In this way, the Earth is considered to be sacred. Air and water, being the source of life, were also cherished. Polluting the soil, water, or air was considered to be a very serious sin.

Zoroastrianism has such customs as praying five times a day, cleaning oneself, celebrating a new year, celebrating the memory of one's ancestors, partaking of sacred drinks, and having teenagers participate in religious customs and weddings.

Praying took place in temples. The man prayed toward the south. Cleaning oneself was a very important custom. A man could not touch dirty creatures and animals (for example, ants or snakes). Zoroastrians were not supposed to soil the source of life. While consuming meat, they cleansed it completely of blood.

In order not to pollute the earth, the bones of a dead man were not simply buried in the ground .They were placed into special vessels—ossuaries. Then, they were placed in a deep pit and covered by a stone. Currently, Persian Zoroastrians bury the deceased in the ground. But before the burying them, they cover the inner walls of the grave with cement and, in this way, prevent the earth from becoming polluted. Zoroastrians in India still perform burial ceremonies as their ancestors did before.

The ceremony when children joined Zoroastrianism was considered to be very significance. The goal of this ceremony was strengthen the faith of a young Zoroastrian in the good deeds and kindness of Ahura Mazda. The ceremony was conducted for children between seven and 15 years old.

Beginning at the age of seven, a child was given a religious education. When a boy was seven years old, he was dressed in a sacred shirt and instructed by his educator to look at the sun (fire). Together, they addressed god Ahura Mazda. The children promised to be devoted to their religion. At the same time, they pledged that they would strive for good ideas, good words and good deeds. When a boy was 15 years old, he wore a sash along his waist. This was the symbol of faith in Zoroastrianism. From the age of 15, young Zoroastrians had to take part in religious ceremonies at the temples.

ZOROASTRIANISM ON LIFE AND DEATH

In Zoroastrianism, the body of a man dies but the soul does not. The soul of a deceased man remains in the body for three days. Then, on the fourth day, it passes to the other world. First, it goes to the peak of Adyta Mountains. Then, it must cross the bridge named "Chinwad."

People who did good deeds cross over the bridge easily, because while they are passing across the bridge it widens. When the soul crosses the Chinwad Bridge it enters Paradise and there the souls wait for doomsday, when they will enter their bodies again.

People who did evil things cannot cross the Chinwad Bridge because the bridge becomes too narrow. A sinful man walking along it falls into the bottomless pit of Hell.

ZOROASTRIANISM ON A MAN'S UPBRINGING AND MORALS

Zarathustra said, "Bringing up a man is the main support of life." Zoroastrians raised a child in three ways: religious and moral upbringing, physical training, and teaching a child to read and write

Religious upbringing continued from age seven to 15. The aim of moral upbringing was to inculcate honesty and good behavior. A diligent human being was considered to be a man who displayed good conduct. Every man must have a profession. Zoroastrianism teaches that a man without a trade cannot live properly. It says that good deeds are manifest in the labor of peasants. A lazy man will die poor.

Zoroastrianism considers that a man should strive to have good thoughts, speak wise words engage in good deeds, to be well bred with high moral qualities. A person with high morals does good deeds for everybody. He will be kinds towards orphans and disabled people .He will respect and show high esteem toward the believers in other religions. He will not engage in bad deeds. He will stay on the right path and not envy others. He will not earn money in immoral ways.

JUDAISM

THE EMERGENCE OF JUDAISM

Judaism is the monotheist religion of the Hebrews. The name of the religion is taken from the name of the tribe of Judah. The strivings of the Hebrews to be united and to create a united state come from the basics of this religion.

In the 10th Century BC, the Hebrews founded their own state for the first time. The tribe of Judah played a decisive part in this. The first dynasty of Hebrew kings came from this tribe

The founder of the Hebrew state was David (1004-965 BC). From that time, all the Hebrews began to pray Yahweh, the god of the Judah tribe. Judaism became a national religion.

King Sula*Iman* (Solomon) built a majestic temple to Yahweh in Jerusalem in the 10th Century BC.

THE FATE OF JUDAISM

In 586 BC, the Babylonians destroyed the Hebrew temple and took the Hebrews into exile. This increased the significance of the temple for the Hebrews. It became their image of salvation and the Hebrews began separating from other nations. Intermarriage between Hebrews and other peoples was strictly forbidden. The reason for this was to preserve the Hebrews as a nation.

In 63 BC, the Roman Empire conquered Palestine. The uprising of the Hebrews for freedom were crushed without mercy. When an uprising was crushed in 70 AD, the Jerusalem temple was destroyed again and in 133 AD the city of Jerusalem was itself destroyed. The Hebrews were persecuted and they went to different countries of the world. But where they went the Hebrews were devoted to their faith and religion. Wherever they went they built their synagogues. And the synagogues at same time were organizations governing Hebrew society.

MOSES IS THE PROPHET OF JUDAISM
How did Moses become the prophet of Judaism?

In the sacred book of Judaism, it says the following: The Hebrews take their origin from Abraham (the supreme father). God made an agreement with Abraham and said to him: "Your name is not Abram but Abraham now. I shall make an agreement with you and your descendants which will be valid for the next generations, too."

The Hebrews believe that God gave to Abraham and his descendants for eternity the territories from the Nile River to the Euphrates.

When Abraham passed away, his property passed to Isaac. Isaac had two twin sons: Isaiah and Jacob. Jacob had 12 children and he loved Joseph most of all his children. Joseph's brothers felt envious and sold Joseph to merchants. But they told their father that Joseph had been eaten by wild animals. The merchants, in turn, sold Joseph to the court of the Egyptian Pharaoh.

After some time, Joseph became a close advisor of the Pharaoh. The reason was that he could interpret dreams very well and he was good at mathematics.

After some years passed, there was a famine in the land of the Hebrews. Some of the Hebrews went to Egypt in search of wheat. At that time, the Egyptian Pharaoh, in accordance with Joseph's prophecy, had laid in a stock of wheat sufficient for seven years.

Fifty years later, Joseph passed away. There was no one who could take his place. Also, the Egyptian Pharaoh had begun persecuting foreigners because they became too numerous. Even newborn babies were killed. The Hebrews were in danger of disappearing completely, so they decided to escape from Egypt.

At that time God sent them a leader. His name was Moses. With the help of the god Yahweh, Moses led the Hebrews out of Egypt.
Yahweh presented Moses with 10 commandments on Mount Sinai:
1. Not to pray to any other gods
2. Not to make graven images
3. Not to swear using the name of God
4. To respect and cherish the sabbath [Saturday] and devote this day to God
5. To respect and cherish one's parents
6. Not to kill
7. Not to commit adultery
8. Not to steal
9. Not to give false testimony
10. Not to covet other people's property

Then Yahweh sent Moses other sacred books of Judaism. And Moses began spreading Yahweh's words—the content of the sacred books—among the Hebrews.

THE SACRED BOOKS OF JUDAISM.
The sacred books of Judaism are the "Old Testament" and the "Talmud" (Learning). The Old Testament (Agreement with God) was written in the old Hebrew language and consists of 39 books. The first five of them are called the five books of Moses—the Pentateuch. These five books are also called the Torah (Law). This is the basis of the Hebrews' religious teaching. The second book of Judaism is the Talmud (Learning).

WHAT DOES JUDAISM TEACH?
Judaism teaches that God created everything in the world in six days. Everything in the world takes place according to the will and wish of God. God created a human being on the sixth day. And a human being takes care of the world.

Judaism teaches that the Hebrews are the nation selected by God. Therefore, God made an agreement with them.

In Judaism, there are the notions of a "divine hero," "a savior," and "a national hero." According to these beliefs, the divine hero will appear one day in the future and liberate Hebrews from tyranny. In Judaism, there is also a belief in "the next world."

SPECIFIC FEATURES OF JUDAISM.

Judaism has very strict requirements. These requirements even regulate the clothes to be worn, meals to be eaten, the order of the day of a Jew. The Jews do not make a step without saying a prayer. The children receive a religious education from the age of five or six.

Judaism forbids its followers to eat the meat of a camel, pig or a rabbit. Meat allowed to be eaten must not be bloody. While sleeping, the Jews must cover their heads with something. While performing religious ceremonies they must wear a cloak over their clothes.

RELIGIOUS CUSTOMS AND HOLIDAYS.

Judaism has religious customs such as praying, celebrating the Sabbath on Saturday, celebrating birthdays, marriage and funeral ceremonies. A Jew who is 30 must pray three times a day—in the morning, in the afternoon and in the evening.

Saturday is considered to be a sacred day in Judaism. God created the world in six days and on the seventh day he rested. The Jews considered Saturday the seventh day.

The observance of the sabbath begins on sundown on Friday. At this time, the celebration ceremony starts with saying prayers in a synagogue or at home and reading odes. Parents say prayers on behalf of their children. On Saturday, Jews do not do any work or cook any meals. They do even not make fires. They wear clothes made of white cloth, which symbolize cleanliness and peace, and read prayers from their sacred books.

After a son is born, his name is announced when he is eight days old. A boy is considered to be a religious adult when he is 13 and a girl when she is 12. A boy of 13 is called "a son of the Testament and the girl of 12 "a daughter of the Testament." From this age on, they are responsible for following religious rules.

The marriage ceremony is especially of significance because Jews look upon marriage as the basis for the continued existence of their religion.

Judaism has a number of holidays. One of the most important is Passover. As related above, God kept the Hebrews safe and sound during their captivity in Egypt when the Egyptian Pharaoh was being punished with plagues. This event took place on the last 10 days of the Hebrew captivity in Egypt.

In addition, Judaism has another holiday called Yom Kippur (the day of atonement). This holiday is devoted to asking forgiveness from God for one's sins. During this holiday, the Hebrews ask God to excuse their sins during a 10-day period.

ISLAM

THE EMERGENCE OF ISLAM

Islam appeared in Arabia in the seventh Century. At that time, the life of Arab society had become very vulgar and petty. Hard drinking, gambling, meanness and debauchery were prominent. Most people had lost their feeling of shame. Women were treated like cattle. Some ill-bred and ignorant fathers buried their newborn daughters alive.

It was necessary to save society from such ignorance and meanness. It was necessary to find the way of salvation.

Also, there was the danger of foreign invasion. In Arabia, no strong state existed that could cope with such a danger. Every Arabian tribe lived separately, keeping to itself. Each of them had its particular god and this was preventing the Arabs from uniting in one state. The Arabian tribes could be united, however, on the basis of a monotheist religion. In this way, Islam emerged.

In Islam, God is called Allah. The Islamic religion acknowledge that Allah is the only God; that one should obey Allah and be faithful with one's whole heart and soul.

The people who accepted Islam and followed its prophet were called Muslims. The prophet of this religion was Muhammad bin Abdullah. He began to propagandize and to spread this new religion in Arabia. From that time, Muhammad bin Abdullah devoted his life to the way of salvation.

Muhammad bin Abdullah could see the mighty force of this religion, which was able to unite the Arabian tribes into one state. So, he fought to create a mighty, united state. After tough struggles in 630, Arabia became a united state. Later, this state entered the history under the name of the Arabian Caliphate.

THE SACRED BOOK OF ISLAM

The sacred book of Islam is called the Qur'an. This means "the recitation." In Islam, the words of this book are considered to be the words of God. The Qur'an was sent through angel Gabriel to Muhammad ibn Abdullah. During the time of Muhammad ibn Abdullah Qur'an was not written down as a separate book. The words of Allah were learned by heart by the companions in-arms of the Prophet. Also, they were written on different pieces of parchment. After the death of Muhammad ibn Abdullah, the Qur'an was compiled as a separate book.

In the Muslim world, the copy of Caliph Uthman's Qur'an is very famous. Uthman ruled the Arabian Caliphate from 644 to 656. He ordered the Qur'an to be compiled as a separate book in 651. Four copies of the Qur'an were made. It is called Mushaf (pages with the cover) but around the world it is famous under the name of "Uthman's Qur'an." It was written on deer skin. One of the copies of "Uthman's Qur'an" is kept in Tashkent. The other three copies are in Cairo, Mecca and Istanbul. The copy of "Uthman's Qur'an" was brought to Tashkent during the reign of Timur. It was kept in Samarkand for several hundred years. In 1869, it was taken to Petersburg and given back to Tashkent in 1923.

In 1989, the government of Uzbekistan passed this book to the Uzbekistan Muslim Board. It is currently kept in the library of the Board.

The Chapters of the Qur'an are called "surah;" the verses of the surahs are called "ayats."

ABOUT THE PROPHET MUHAMMAD

As mentioned above, Muhammad ibn Abdullah is considered to be the prophet of Islam. According to the teachings of Islam, Allah told him to spread the Islamic religion among people. Muhammad was born in Mecca in 570. When he was two months old, his father passed away. When he was six years old, his mother died. Muhammad became an orphan and was brought up by his grandfather Abdul Mutallib. Two years later, his grandfather passed away and Muhammad became was a dependent in the family of his uncle Abu Talib.

Abu Talib was a merchant and he taught his nephew this trade. Muhammad was a hard-working and very clever boy. As a teenager, he went to different places with trade caravans. This activity taught him to live and survive in the conditions of the desert. Later, he worked as a herdsman.

Muhammad was brought up as a man of great intellect and high morals. When he was 24, he won the name Muhammad Amin, which meant "devoted", "open-hearted." When he was 25, he married a woman named Khadijah. They had six children: two sons and four daughters. Five of them did not live long. Only their daughter Fatima lived for a long time. She was a very highly esteemed person. When his uncle was in a financial difficulty, Muhammad brought up his son Ali and Ali eventually married Muhammad's daughter Fatima.

MUHAMMAD IBN ABDULLAH'S ACTIVITY AS PROPHET

As it is written in the books of Islam, the prophethood of Muhammad ibn Abdullah began in 610. Islamic scholars believe that Allah chooses a prophet among the people. Allah does not speak to human beings because a human being cannot stand speaking to Allah directly. Therefore, Allah sends his words to the prophet through an angel.

When Muhammad ibn Abdullah was sent the first message he was 40 years old. In the history of Islam, this night is called "the night of destiny" ("Laylat ul qadr"). From this day, the 40-year-old Muhammad ibn Abdullah became the Prophet—a messenger of Allah to whom the sacred book, the Qur'an, was sent. Muhammad received various parts of the Qur'an during a period of 23 years.

When Islam began to be propagated, the population of Mecca became divided into two groups. They were called the faithful—mu'min-muslims—and the non-believers—mushriks. The Muslims were those who believed that Allah is the only God and that Muhammad was his prophet. The non-believers were those who did not believe in Islam. The struggle between them continued more than 20 years. Even Muhammad and his companions-in-arms had to move from Mecca to Medina in 622. In the history of Islam, this is called the "hijra," the migration.

In Medina, Muhammad created an ummah (community), that is, a city-state. In 630, the city of Mecca also became Muhammad's followers. In this way, the Arabian tribes were united in one state with Muhammad as its ruler. Muhammad passed away on June 8, 632, at the age of 63.

<u>ISLAM BECOMES A WORLD RELIGION</u>

When Muhammad died, the Muslim state began to be ruled by caliphs. From 632 to 661, four caliphs (Abu Bakr Siddiq, Umar, Uthman and Ali) reigned. During this time, Islam spread all over the world. In the eighth Century, Islam became the religion of present-day Central Asia.

Today, Muslims are found on every continent. The population of the world is now more than 6.5 billion. About 1.5 billion people are Muslims. Most Central Asians are Muslims. In the West, there are more and more Muslims. For example, there are six million Muslims in the United States. France, Great Britain and Germany each has more than two million Muslims. In Canada, there are 500,000.

<u>ISLAMIC TEACHING, CUSTOMS AND HOLIDAYS</u>

Islamic teaching

There is notion of faith or *"Iman"* in Islamic teaching. *Iman* consists of seven dogmas. They are belief in Allah, angels, prophets, sacred books, the Judgment Day, fate and life after death.

1. First, Allah created the world and then all the creatures. Everything takes place according to His will. The Judgment Day will also be held according to Allah's will. Allah has existed forever. Allah was not created by anybody. Allah is one, alone. There is nothing that Allah doesn't know. Allah does not make any errors or have any shortcomings.

2. Angels are creatures of Allah that can't be seen. They are very obedient to Allah. They are sinless and were created from light rays. They do what Allah orders them.

3. Prophets are Allah's ambassadors to mankind. They taught humans the rules of the religion. They urge people to do good deeds. They follow Allah's will. They are chosen from among people.

4. The sacred books consist of Allah's words. Allah sent these sacred books to Moses, David, Jesus and Muhammad. The Qur'an consists of Allah's words.

5. The Judgment Day is the day when there is nobody left except Allah and the human beings that Allah chooses.

6. Fate is the pre-ordained occurrence of all good and bad deeds; the fate of a man is determined beforehand by Allah.

7. Judgment Day is the day when the good deeds and bad deeds of people will judged. This day will be a happy one for good people and terrible for bad people. Good people will pass over the Sirat bridge and enter Paradise. Bad people will not pass over it and will go to Hell.

Islamic rites
In Islam there are five rites to be fulfilled. They are:
  * *Shahadah*;
  * Praying;
  * Keeping a fast;
  * Paying *zakat* (charitable tax);
  * Going to a pilgrimage to Mecca.

What is the *shahadah*? It is the pronouncement that there is no god but Allah and Muhammad is his prophet. In Islamic countries, you hear these words every day. Islam requires that every Muslim pronounce the *shahadah*.

Praying is reading ayats from the Qur'an and saying odes in honor of Allah. It is one of the most significant ways to maintain a religious mood in Muslims. As it is written in the sacred book, Allah created the entire world and everything in it for the mankind. Therefore Allah made saying prayers a must to express their gratefulness and to remember him.

Praying is done five times a day. The Qur'an says that praying will prevent people from doing bad things. Islam teaches that praying five times a day is like being received by Allah five times.

Fasting is not eating or drinking from sunrise until sunset. In Islam, fasting is mandatory during the month of Ramadan for everybody who is not traveling and who is in good health. People who are ill, traveling, or elderly are not obliged to fast. In Islam, one should spend the month of Ramadan being grateful to Allah. According to the opinion of Muslim scholars, fasting is a divine test for human beings. It teaches a man to be patient and, being patient, he or she will reach Allah. Fasting is a means of improving a man, also, because fasting requires people not to offend anyone, to stop telling lies and to forego doing bad deeds. At the same time, during fasting, the internal organs rest for a month.

Wealthy Muslims must give *zakat* (charitable taxes) to the poor, orphans and handicapped. *Zakat* is very important in financially supporting the poor, orphans and handicapped; therefore it is mentioned next to praying (*namaz*) in the Qur'an. A wealthy man must give a part of his property, as ordered by Allah. In doing so, the rich will purify their wealth and property. The *zakat* is composed of 2.5% of a person's property.

In addition to being spent for the poor and handicapped, *zakat* is spent for *zakat* collectors, for debtors who became indebted while doing good deeds, for travelers and for the way of Allah (for building mosques, *madrassas*, and orphanages). One can give a pension, but not *zakat*, to people of other religions, one's parents, grandparents, sons, daughters, grandchildren and wife.

Hajj (an Arabic word meaning pilgrimage) means going to Mecca, the sacred city of Islam, during the last month of the Muslim calendar. During the pilgrimage, one fulfills various religious custom and rites. Mecca is located in the territory of present-day Saudi Arabia.

Why do Muslims make this pilgrimage? In Mecca, there is a building called the Kaaba. As is stated in the Qur'an, the Kaaba is the house of Allah. The house was built by the prophet Abraham and his son Ishmael. Muslim scholars say that Allah ordered Muslims who can afford it to go travel his house and pray there, and then to go to Arafat Mountain and pray there. Every year, Muslims visit Mecca to fulfill their pilgrimage duty. They beg Allah to forgive them for their errors, sins and bad deeds.

The millions of people performing the Hajj rites are all dressed in the same clothes. One can not distinguish a king from a common man. The fact that all the people are equal before Allah is manifest in this ceremony. After performing all the rites, Hajjis come to the city of Medina, where they perform a pilgrimage of the mosque of the Prophet Muhammad and read prayers in this mosque. That ends the Hajj.

Besides these five main rites, there is also *janaza* (saying prayers for the deceased before burial), sunnah, marriage and other rites.

Islamic holidays
Islam has holidays, as do other religions. The most important ones are Eid al-Fitr and Eid al-Adha.

As discussed, fasting occurs during the month of Ramadan. At the end of the month, the Eid al-Fitr or breaking of the fast is celebrated. This is an occasion for Muslims to express their joy and pleasure to each other on the occasion of the fulfillment of their duty to keep the fast. On the day of Eid al-Fitr, prayers are read and, after praying, Muslims great and congratulate each other.

On Eid al-Adha, an offering is made to slaughter a sheep as the sign of being close to Allah. Islamic scholars explain the origin of holiday as follows: the prophet Abraham was willing to slaughter his son Ishmael for the sake of Allah. But the knife did not cut Ishmael's neck, due to the will of Allah. Allah saved Ishmael's life due to his devotion. Allah then sent a ram to Abraham and ordered to slaughter it instead of his son.

On the final day of the Hajj, people slaughter a sheep in memory of this on Eid al-Adha. The meat of a slaughtered sheep is distributed among the members of the family, relatives and neighbors. Eid prayers are read. Relatives, friends and neighbors greet each other and congratulate each other on the holiday.

Islam Law (Shari'ah)
Shari'ah is the collection of religious laws and regulations to be followed by Muslims. In short, Shari'ah is the code of Islamic law. There are many different types of laws. They consist of laws concerning religion, civil affairs, property, inheritance, debt, family and marriage, and criminal affairs.

For 1400 years, Shari'ah has been regulating the life of society in Islamic countries. In the countries where the life of a society is not regulated by Islamic law, the Muslims of these countries carry out religious rites in accordance with Shari'ah.

Where there is no law, there is disorder. In states with a lax legal system, disorder reigns. So the legal system must be a priority for every state.

THE PRIMARY SCHOOL LEVEL

A Kyrgyz expert in Islamic affairs, Dr. Orozbec Moldaliev, proposed the following curriculum for religious lessons in Muslim primary schools:

Elementary concepts—for grades 1-4

1st year, 1st Quarter, 32 hours
The ABC Book of Faith:

Lesson 1: *Goals and objectives of the subject of the "Faith Lessons:"*
Introduction to the subject of "Faith Lessons"
Concept of Faith

Lesson 2: *Ethics of greeting, its meaning and types*
Explanation of the greeting process
Explanation of the origin of greeting and its meaning

Lesson 3: *School is our home*
Explanation of the word "school"
Schools are our wealth

Lesson 4: *Teachers should serve as an example of virtue*
Explanation of the word "teacher" and what he or she is
Respect for the teacher

Lesson 5: *Making friends*
What is a real friend?
Who is a real friend?

Lesson 6: *What is faith?*
Faith in the existence of God
The origin of religious faith

Lesson 7: Recap of the material of the quarter

1st year, 2nd Quarter
Being Clean and Disciplined

Lesson 1: *Cleanness is a part of faith*
Wash your face and clean your teeth in the morning
Take a shower every week

Lesson 2: *Keep your clothes clean*
Be always dressed in clean and neat clothes
Do not play in dirty places

Lesson 3: *Keep your words clean*
Do not say words that you would not like to hear
Do not say bad words or gossip behind the back of other people

Lesson 4: *Keep your surroundings clean*
Keep the surroundings of your house clean
Pay attention to the cleanliness of the school and classroom

Lesson 5: *Let your heart be pure*
Keep a good and pure intention
Have a good opinion of other people

Lesson 6: *Be disciplined*
Be disciplined at home, school and in society
Keep your room clean and learn to put your things in order

Lesson 7: Recap of the material of the quarter
1ˢᵗ year, 3ʳᵈ Quarter
Parents are the Dearest

Lesson 1: *Respect for parents*
Show respect to grandparents and other relatives
Lesson 2: *What is it mean to be excessively spoiled by parents?*
Lesson 3: *Praying for the souls of late parents is a type of ethics*
Lesson 4: *Justify your mother's care!*
Lesson 5: *Do not let others say a bad word about your parents*
Lesson 6: *Help your grandparents, parents, sisters and brothers*
Lesson 7: Recap of the material of the quarter

1ˢᵗ year, 4ᵗʰ Quarter
Homeland

Lesson 1: *The homeland is sacred*
What is the homeland?
Lesson 2: *Why did heroes defend their homeland?*
How will you defend your homeland?
Lesson 3: *Nature and ourselves*
Our attitude to nature
Lesson 4: *Animals are our friends*
Lesson 5: *Our close neighbors*
Lesson 6: *The significance of a neighbor in Islam*
Lesson 7: *Do not trouble your neighbors*
Lesson 8: Recap of the material of the quarter

2nd year, 1st Quarter, 32 hours
Faith is a Source of Humaneness

Lesson 1: *The meaning of the word faith and its requirements*
Lesson 2: *Faith is the most valuable thing in a human being*
Lesson 3: *Show respect towards the elderly and the young*
Lesson 4: *Conscience and shame*
Lesson 5: *What is honor? A boy who defends honor is conscientious*
Lesson 6: *Cleanness and purity are sources of faith*
Lesson 7: *Mercifulness and kindness*
Lesson 8: Recap of the material of the quarter

2nd year, 2nd Quarter
All Muslims are Brothers (All those who believe in Allah are brothers)

Lesson 1: *Brotherhood in faith*
Lesson 2: *Kinship and brotherhood*
Lesson 3: *Let us consider all people as friends and brothers*
Lesson 4: *Ethics of respect toward parents*
Lesson 5: *Have the blessing of parents*
Lesson 6: *The mother is the keeper of the home fire; the mother is holy*
Lesson 7: *Good intentions and generosity*
Lesson 8: Recap of the materials of the quarter

2nd year, 3rd Quarter
Who is a Prophet?

Lesson 1: *Explanation of what the prophets are*
Lesson 2: *A brief biography of the Prophet Muhammad (PBUH)*
Lesson 3: *Let us take the friendship as an example of virtue*
Lesson 4: *Favorite friends of the Prophet*
Lesson 5: *Holy Abu Bakr al-Siddiq*
Lesson 6: *Holy Umar*
Lesson 7: *Holy Othman*
Lesson 8: *Holy Ali*
Lesson 9: Recap of the materials of the quarter

2nd year, 4th Quarter
The Holiday is a Joy for All the People

Lesson 1: *What are religious holiday and the holiday?*
Lesson 2: *Holiday of Orozo ait (Eid al-Fitr) and its meaning*
Lesson 3: *Holiday of Kurban ait (Eid al-Adha)*
Lesson 4: *Origin of Kurban ait and Kurban*
Lesson 5: *The holy day in Islam—Friday*
Lesson 6: *National holidays*
Lesson 7: Recap of the material of the quarter

3rd year, 1st Quarter, 34 hours
Faith and Ethics

Lesson 1: *Islam's ethics are relevant to all mankind*
Lesson 2: *Faith, ethics*
Faith in God
Being tolerant
Lesson 3: *Earn an honest livelihood*
Lesson 4: *Be on friendly terms with all people*
Lesson 5: *Do not have bad intentions*
Do not steal
Do not gossip
Do not abuse others
Lesson 6: *Let us help the poor, orphans and widows*
Lesson 7: *Learn the prayers of faith*
Lesson 8: *Explanation of the prayers of faith*
Lesson 9: Recap of the materials of the quarter

3rd year, 2nd Quarter
Customs, Traditions and Religion

Lesson 1: *When a child is born, azan (call to prayer) is made; the parents' duty is to give the child a Muslim name*

Lesson 2: *Your cradle*
Traditions of the cradle and circumcision
Lesson 3: *How to wash, eat, come in and go out of the house, lie down and stand up*
Lesson 4: *Having the blessings of the elderly*
Lesson 5: *The ethics of praying*
Prayer is a favor for good deeds
Pray for the souls of the departed
Knowing how to pray
Lesson 6: *The combination of tradition and faith*
Lesson 7: *A lie never helps*
Make comments on this statement
Lesson 8: *What is honor?*
The honor of Kyrgyz heroes
Lesson 9: Recap of the materials of the quarter

3rd year, 3rd Quarter
The Quest to Obtain Knowledge and Science is Everyone's Duty

Lesson 1: *Science leads a person to light from darkness*
Lesson 2: *Ignorance is caused by an absence of knowledge*
Lesson 3: *It is not a shame to what you don't know*
Lesson 4: *Praise for science by the Prophet Muhammad (PBUH)*
Lesson 5: *Keeping school supplies clean helps science*
Lesson 6: *The importance of sleeping less, talking less and being clean*
Lesson 7: *The prosperity of the homeland is in the hands of the educated*
Lesson 8: *Respect for the homeland comes from faith*
Lesson 9: Recap of the materials of the quarter

3rd year, 4th Quarter

Lesson 1: *Fundamentals of Faith in Islam*
- Faith in God
- Faith in the Prophet (PBUH)
- Faith in the book
- Faith in angels

- Faith in the afterworld
- Faith in destiny

Lesson 2: *There is no compulsion in faith*
Lesson 3: *Faith is a link between God and worship*
Lesson 4: *Food earned honestly is blessed food*
Lesson 5: *Doing good deeds is a form of worship*
Lesson 6: *Work is a key to happiness*
Lesson 7: Recap of the materials of the quarter

4th year, 1st Quarter, 34 hours
Ethics, Ibadah (worship) and Religion

Lesson 1: *Understanding of the oneness of Allah means learning the Tauhid prayer*
Lesson 2: *Understanding the concept of Islam*
Lesson 3: *Biography of the Holy Muhammad (PBUH)*
Lesson 4: *The holy book of Islam is the Qur'an*
Lesson 5: *Islam is a religion of love*
Lesson 6: *Islam is a religion of peace*
Lesson 7: *What is ibadah? Worship should be done only for Allah*
Lesson 8: *Ibadah improves ethics*
Lesson 9: *Praying is ibadah*
Lesson 10: Recap of the materials of the quarter

4th year, 2nd Quarter
Love for the Homeland is Based on Faith

Lesson 1: *My homeland is my golden cradle*
Lesson 2: *Nature is a gift of the Creator*
Lesson 3: *Being proud of the homeland*
Lesson 4: *The one who pollutes water will be condemned*
Lesson 5: *Appreciate youthfulness*
Lesson 6: Recap of the materials of the quarter

4ᵗʰ year, 3ʳᵈ Quarter
Explanation of Permitted and Forbidden Things

Lesson 1: *The difference between the permitted and the forbidden*
Lesson 2: *Rudeness causes regret*
Lesson 3: *Everything that harms the health is haram (forbidden)*
cigarettes, drugs, alcohol, theft, violence
Lesson 4: *Politeness and humility are essential ethical values*
Lesson 5: *Accepting fair criticism is wise and courageous*
Lesson 6: *Where indifference leads:*
Indifference extinguishes responsibility
Lesson 7: *Getting angry and quarreling indicates a lack of self-control and carelessness*
Lesson 8: *Telling lies and slanders is impudence*
Lesson 9: *Greed, envy and bad intentions*
Lesson 10: Recap of the materials of the quarter

4ᵗʰ year, 4ᵗʰ Quarter
Family and Cleanliness

Lesson 1: *The responsibility to respect parents*
Lesson 2: *Our attitude toward the elderly, sick, weak and orphans*
Lesson 3: *Let's keep clean our house, school and environment*
Assist in cleaning the house
Keep the classroom clean
Do not shout or spit in the street
Lesson 4: *Keeping one's words under control*
Do not say words that you do not want to hear
Joke moderately and don't say bad words
Don't call bad names
Lesson 5: *Allah and people like those who keep themselves clean*
Lesson 6: *Faith and science purify our hearts*
Time is as valuable as gold
Lesson 7: Recap of the materials of the quarter

Advanced concepts—for grades 5-11

5th year, 1st Quarter, 34 hours
Ethics and Faith

Lesson 1: *Ethics of greeting*
Lesson 2: *Ethics of behavior in the street, social places and mosques*
Ethics of asking permission
Ethics of talking
Ethics of hospitality
Ethics of eating
Lesson 4: *Politeness and generosity*
Lesson 5: *Requirements of faith (What does the expression of faith in Allah mean?)*
Lesson 6: *Worship is a basis of ethics*
Lesson 7: *Keep your honor from a young age; modesty*
Lesson 8: *Doing good is a form of worship*
Lesson 9: Recap of the materials of the quarter

5th year, 2nd Quarter
Kindness and Religion

Lesson 1: *Why and to whom should we give alms, zakat (charity)?*
Lesson 2: *Types of kindness*
zakat
orozo, bitir
ushur
alms
charity meal offered to God (*ihsan*, the good)
Lesson 3: *Think of the statement: "The friend comes back, the enemy leaves"*
Lesson 4: *Rewards of kindness*
Lesson 5: *The meaning of the word ";eligion;" what is religion?*
Lesson 6: *Need of a religion for the human race*
Lesson 7: *Learning the basics of the Islamic religion*
Lesson 8: *Islam is a religion of good ethics*
Lesson 9: Recap of the materials of the quarter

5th year, 3rd Quarter
A Person's Noble Qualities are Signs of Faith

Lesson 1: *Noble qualities are the main instruments that will bring happiness*
Lesson 2: *If you respect otherst, you will be respected*
Lesson 3: *A truly humble person will never harm*
Lesson 4: *Politeness, humility and hospitality grace a person*
Lesson 5: *Accepting fair criticism is wise and courageous*
Lesson 6: *A good word is good for the heart and life*
Lesson 7: *Keep promises; decisiveness*
Lesson 8: *Returning the thing you borrowed to its owner*
Lesson 9: Recap of the materials of the quarter

5th year, 4th Quarter
The First Forefather Adam and his Descendants

Lesson 1: *The story about the Holy Father Adam and Mother Eve*
Lesson 2: *The story of the Prophets Enoch, Noah, Hud, Saleh*
Lesson 3: *The story of the Prophets Abraham, Lot, Ishmael, Isaac, Jacob, Joseph, Job, Jethro*
Lesson 4: *The story of the Prophets Moses, Aaron, David, Solomon, Elias, Ezekiel, Jonah, Zacharias, Isaiah, Jesus Christ*
Stories of the prophets
Lesson 5: *The Holy Prophet Muhammad (PBUH) and his life*
Lesson 6: *The time of the Holy Prophet Muhammad (PBUH) and Islam*
Lesson 7: Recap of the materials of the quarter

6th year, 1st Quarter, 34 hours
Faith is a Source of Enhancement

Lesson 1: *Faith prayer and its essence*
Lesson 2: *Shame is a true mirror of the heart*
Shame always brings good to a person
Lesson 3: *Ignorance is a sign of unhappiness (arrogance, lies and deeds that Allah does not like)*

152

Lesson 4: *"The result of work depends on its intentions" (detailed explanation of the hadith)*

Lesson 5: *Cleanliness is a part of faith*

lesson 6: *Ethics depends on character*

Lesson 7: *The person who admits his guilt and repents is equal to an innocent person*

Lesson 8: *Modesty and gentleness mean the greatness of a person (tolerance)*

Lesson 9: *The one who commits violence is as guilty as a criminal*

Lesson 10: Recap of the materials of the quarter

6th year, 2nd Quarter
Science is Essential for the Intelligence of a Nation
The Level of Knowledge of Nation

Lesson 1: *Discuss the statement of the Prophet (PBUH): "Search for knowledge, even in China."*

Lesson 2: *Explanation of the science of hadith; types of hadiths*

Lesson 3: *Science and skills are most valuable*
"My dear children, obtain knowledge and skills. They will develop your life."

Lesson 4: *Wasting time is the greatest form of mischief (laziness is the door to poverty)*

Lesson 5: *The ethics of obtaining knowledge*

Lesson 6: *Learning the rules of Islamic Shari'ah*

Lesson 7: Recap of the materials of the quarter

6th year, 3rd Quarter
Ethics of Behavior in the Family

Lesson 1: *Discuss the statement: "Obeying your father means obeying God."*

Lesson 2: *Lukman Hakim's statements about obedience to parents and Allah*

Lesson 3: *Depending on his education, a child treats his parents well or poorly*

Lesson 4: *Discuss the hadith: "Youth is another type of foolery."*

Lesson 5: *Wastefulness is a beginning of a life of poverty (wastefulness in the family)*

Lesson 6: *A good boy and girl always support their parents and do not utter a single bad word against them*
Lesson 7: *The stories of Yusuf aleihis salam and his brother*
Lesson 8: *The instructions of the father*
Lesson 9: *Let the young have work and the old have wealth*
Lesson 10: Recap of the materials of the quarter

6th year, 4th Quarter
Faith, Ibadah (worship) and Religion

Lesson 1: *Introduction to the 40 obligations of Islam*
Lesson 2: *Types of verdicts in Islam*
Lesson 3: *Concept of ibadah in Islam and its types*
Ibadah means worship
Any good is *ibadah*
Lesson 4: *Life in the grave is called "Alamuh barzah"*
Lesson 5: *Explanation of the afterworld, the field of makhshar*
Lesson 6: *On Paradise and Hell*
Lesson 7: Recap of the materials of the quarter

7th year, 1st Quarter, 34 hours
Influence of Islam on the National Culture (Kyrgyz Example)

Lesson 1: *The Great Silk Road and the Kyrgyz land*
Lesson 2: *The story of the battle of the 750s. The holy Issyk-Kul*
Lesson 3: *Establishment of Karahanid state. Burana, Ozgon architectural monuments*
Lesson 4: *Yusuf Balasagun. Excerpt from his book "Blessed Knowledge"*
Lesson 5: *Mahmud Kashgari's book "The Dictionary of Turkic Languages"*
Lesson 6: *The "Manas" epic and its religious concepts*
Lesson 7: *Outstanding Kyrgyz people (Moldo Niyaz, Moldo Kylych, Kalygul, Arstanbek, Jenijok, Toktogul, Barpy)*
Lesson 8: *The Soviet period and independence*
Lesson 9: Recap of the materials of the quarter

154

7th year, 2nd Quarter
The Permitted and Forbidden Things are Obvious

Lesson 1: *The serious sins in Shari'ah zina,* prostitution
murder theft violence gossip (*gybat*) (saying bad words behind the back of people)
taking bribes
Lesson 2: *Discussion of the hadith: "Lies will never help. Liars are not my followers."*
Lesson 3: *Do not have bad intentions. Make your intentions fair, as this is necessary for your success*
Lesson 4: *Earn an honest livelihood*
Lesson 5: *A courageous man finds honor through work*
Lesson 6: *Wastefulness is a hidden fire of life*
Lesson 7: *All bad things are caused by the tongue*
Lesson 8: *Whoever spoils his heart will spoil his religion*
Lesson 9: Recap of the materials of the quarter

7th year, 3rd Quarter
Paradise is under the Foot of Mothers

Lesson 1: *The role of the girl in the family*
Lesson 2: *Mother's care. The mother is the keeper of the home fire*
Lesson 3: *The family of the holy Prophet Muhammad (PBUH)*
Lesson 4: *A girl should be warned in 40 areas*
Lesson 5: *Calling an innocent woman a prostitute is a sin*
Lesson 6: *A good wife is wealth*
A bad wife is torture
Lesson 7: *Paradise is under the foot of mothers.*

7th year, 4th Quarter
Combination of National Customs and Traditions with Religion

Lesson 1: *The traditions of celebration of the cradle*
Circumcision

Lesson 2: *The past and modern traditions of marrying daughters—marriage brokers, presenting earrings*
Lesson 3: *Rituals related to the marriage of a son (covering the head of a daughter-in-law with a white scarf, etc.)*
Lesson 4: *Shari'ah rules of marriage ceremony*
Lesson 5: *Commemoration means remembering the departed*
Lesson 6: *Knowing the ways of funerals. Combining national traditions with Islamic rules*
Lesson 7: *Visiting an ill person*
Lesson 8: *The responsibility of a child to parents*
Lesson 9: Recap of the materials of the quarter

8th year, 1st Quarter
Preparation for Family Life

Lesson 1: *What is love?*
Lesson 2: *Learning how to choose a husband/wife*
Lesson 3: *What kind of father will I be? (reflection)*
Lesson 4: *What kind of mother will I be? (reflection)*
Lesson 5: *What are the reasons for divorce?*
Lesson 6: *What are the roles of the daughter-in-law and son-in-law?*
Lesson 7: *Reflection on the roles of father and mother*
Lesson 8: *The family is a small state. The state is a large family (reflection)*
Lesson 9: Recap of the materials of the quarter

8th year, 2nd Quarter
Follow your Conscience and Justice

Lesson 1: *The conscious and tolerant person*
Lesson 2: *If you are satisfied with the good given by God, it will grow*
Lesson 3: *The just people of the ancient Arabs (excerpts from stories of the Holy Umar, Holy Umar bin Abdulaziz)*
Lesson 4: *Discussion of the just rules in Islam*
Lesson 5: *Generosity; excerpts from stories of generosity of Hootamtay*
Lesson 6: *Hypocrisy and its results*

Lesson 7: *The one practicing sympathy will receive sympathy*
Lesson 8: *A brave hero has a brave heart*
Lesson 9: Recap of the materials of the quarter

8th year, 3rd Quarter
Homeland is a Holy Land (Example of Kyrgyzstan)

Lesson 1: *My homeland is Kyrgyzstan*
Lesson 2: *The independence of the homeland is a guarantee of consciousness*
Lesson 3: *It is an honor to give one's life for the homeland*
Lesson 4: *We should be the owners of the culture that makes us one nation*
Lesson 5: *The honor of my homeland is my honor*
Lesson 6: *Our history is our wealth*
Lesson 7: Recap of the materials of the quarter

8th year, 4th Quarter
Religious Days, Evening Parties and Holidays

Lesson 1: *Every religion has important days, evening parties and holidays*
Lesson 2: *Friday (Friday prayers, Friday sermons)*
Lesson 3: *The birthday of the Holy Prophet (PBUH)*
Lesson 4: *The holiday of Orozo ait (Eid al-Fitr) and Holy night*
Lesson 5: *Mirage evening party, the holiday of Kurban ait (Eid al-Adha)*
Lesson 6: *The evening parties Barat, Ashura*
Lesson 7: Recap of the materials of the quarter

9th year, 1st Quarter
Faith and History

Lesson 1: *Wealth and its final end*
Lesson 2: *The harm of greed*
Lesson 3: *How to prevent evil?*
Lesson 4: *Making apologies and its benefits*
Lesson 5: *The benefits of repentance*
Lesson 6: *The realization of dreams*
Lesson 7: *Mercifulness and generosity*
Lesson 8: *How to honor the legitimate rights of your wife*

Lesson 9: *If you want to have the respect of your children*
Lesson 10: Recap of the materials of the quarter

9th year, 2nd Quarter
Humaneness

Lesson 1: *Calling for good and preventing evil*
Lesson 2: *Keeping promises*
Lesson 3: *Not to oppose the will*
Lesson 4: *Mercifulness and kindness*
Lesson 5: *Saying bad words behind the backs of other people and results of gossip*
Lesson 6: *Staying in touch with relatives; the rights of parents*
Lesson 7: *Beneficence toward parents*

9th year, 3rd Quarter
The Negative Sides of Life

Lesson 1: *Origins of boasting and impudence and their harm*
Lesson 2: *Results of greed and envy*
Lesson 3: *The ways to eliminate bad character*
Lesson 4: *The harm caused by suspicion*
Lesson 5: *The results of stinginess*
Lesson 6: *The bad sides of wastefulness*
Lesson 7: *The results of cruelty and instigation*
Lesson 8: *Stubbornness and shamelessness*
Lesson 9: *Haste and impatience*
Lesson 10: *The results of revenge and enmity*

9th year, 4th Quarter
The Mind of Person Shows in his Tongue

Lesson 1: *A spoiled tongue spoils the heart*
Lesson 2: *Too long a tongue harms the head*
Lesson 3: *The tongue is the happiness of man*

Lesson 4: *The tongue is a key to the heart*
Lesson 5: *The tongue leads a man to be cursed*
Lesson 6: *Everyone finds happiness from his tongue*
Lesson 7: *The ways of controlling the tongue and its benefits*

10th year, 1st Quarter
Nature and Religion

Lesson 1: *Nature and the Qur'an*
Lesson 2: *The origin of the world*
Lesson 3: *The movements of the Sun, Moon and the Earth*
Lesson 4: *Oxygen and atoms*
Lesson 5: *The creation of everything in pairs*
Lesson 6: *Balance in nature*
Lesson 7: *The resemblance of the animal and avian world to the human world*
Lesson 8: *The development of embryos*
Lesson 9: *On spirit*
Lesson 10: Recap of the materials of the quarter

10th year, 2nd Quarter
Religion and Secular science

Lesson 1: *Science calls for faith*
Lesson 2: *Which sciences does Islam call for?*
Lesson 3: *Western scholars on Islamic culture*
Lesson 4: *The opinion of Western scholars on Islam*
Lesson 5: *Statements of Western scholars on Islamic humaneness*
Lesson 6: *Islam and spiritual life*
Lesson 7: *The world needs spiritual culture*
Lesson 8: *The spiritual rules of other religions*

10th year, 3rd Quarter
Education and Worldview

Lesson 1: *A materialistic view on the world and its influence*

Lesson 2: *An attitude of a person toward the world*
Lesson 3: *The advantage of the afterworld*
Lesson 4: *The world consists of tests*
Lesson 5: *The causes of pomp*
Lesson 6: *What attracts man?*
Lesson 7: *Tolerance, forgiveness, generosity and their types*
Lesson 8: *It is necessary to associate with good people and avoid bad people*
Lesson 9: *Being attracted by lust and arrogance*
Lesson 10: *Conformity and shamelessness*

10th year, 4th Quarter
Wise Instructions and Advice

Lesson 1: *The instructions of the book "Blessed Knowledge" by Yusuf Balasagun*
Lesson 2: *The instructions of Moldo Niyaz*
Lesson 3: *The instructions of Arstanbek Builash uulu*
Lesson 4: *The instructions of Jenijok*
Lesson 5: *The instructions of Moldo Kylych*
Lesson 6: *The instructions of Nur Moldo*
Lesson 7: *The instructions of Moldo Abdurahhim*

11th year, 1st Quarter
Faith and History

Lesson 1: *What is faith ? Who are those with and without faith ?*
Lesson 2: *The history of father Adam and mother Eve and the genealogy of mankind*
Lesson 3: *The origin of fasting, prayer, zakat, hajj and their benefits for society*
Lesson 4: *Whom and what should we worship?*
Lesson 5: *Islam and other religions*
Lesson 6: *Branches of Islam*
Lesson 7: *The concept of prophets*
Lesson 8: *History of the prophets*
Lesson 9: *What religion is a scientific religion?*
Lesson 10: *Biography of the Prophet Muhammad (PBUH)*

160

11ᵗʰ year, 2ⁿᵈ Quarter
Life and Death

Lesson 1: *Being afraid of the Creator and its benefits*
Lesson 2: *Forgetting the Creator and its causes*
Lesson 3: *Obedience to the Creator and following his messengers*
Lesson 4: *The Devil and his enmity towards mankind*
Lesson 5: *Fornication and its threat to society*
Lesson 6: *Hell and its tortures*
Lesson 7: *The benefits of avoiding sin and sinfulness*
Lesson 8: *Paradise and happiness in Paradise*
Lesson 9: *The afterlife and its stories*
Lesson 10: *The scientific justifications for resurrection*

11ᵗʰ year, 3ʳᵈ Quarter
The Best Way of life

Lesson 1: *The value of science and educated people*
Lesson 2: *The results of ignorance*
Lesson 3: *Morality*
Lesson 4: *A child's responsibility to act well towards his parents*
Lesson 5: *Respect for the master and the responsibilities of a disciple*
Lesson 6: *If you do not forget about death, you will not forget about yourself*
Lesson 7: *The results of forbidden deeds and the negative aspects of arrogance*

11ᵗʰ year, 3ʳᵈ Quarter
If You Want to Be an Honorable Person
Lesson 1: *Be intellectual, conscientious, and do not be hypocritical*
Lesson 2: *The results of humiliating orphans and widows*
Lesson 3: *Scientific justifications for the benefits of prayer*
Lesson 4: *The rights of a wife with respect to her husband*
Lesson 5: *The rights of a husband with respect to his wife*
Lesson 6: *The rewards when neighbors help each other and help the needy*
Lesson 7: *The relationship between Muslims and peoples of other religions*

THE VIEWS OF OTHER KYRGYZ EDUCATORS ON TEACHING RELIGIOUS SUBJECTS IN MUSLIM SCHOOLS

The ideas of other Kyrgyz educators about teaching religion lessons in Muslim schools have been outlined at the Web site of the American Foreign Policy Council (www.afpc.org) by Imam Muslim Hajji of the Bishkek Islamic University, in his article *Lessons of Iman (Faith)*.[200] A condensed version of his article follows.

According to Imam Muslim Hajji, the basis of the traditional Muslim educational system lies in memorizing the Qur'an, the hadiths (stories from the life of the Prophet Muhammad), various *tafsirs* (commentaries) on the holy texts, and so on. At primary Muslim schools (*kuttab*), children learn the Qur'an by heart, and in mosques students study the commentaries of instructors.

Many educational institutions provide only studies of works written by Hanbali theological scholars as well as the doctrine of "monotheistic" ideology, as Wahhabism —so-called "pure" Islam—understands it. They pay practically no attention to scholars from other religious-legal Sunni schools of thought, or provide very limited information on their works. The result is that growing generations of young people are convinced that only they are "correct" Muslims. Other believers are considered to be "disbelievers." According to some extremist ideologists, Muslims who do not embrace Wahhabism are considered to be even worse than "disbelievers," because disbelievers are not familiar with the teachings of Islam, which exonerates them to some degree, whereas non-Wahhabis are familiar with the doctrine of al-Wahhab but do not embrace it, making their lack of belief in it even more reproachable.

Furthermore, the alliance between repressive regimes in some Muslim countries and conservative religious theologians has generated interpretations of Islam that are favorable to the authorities, but which restrict freedom of thought, the free exchange of information, and the participation of women in public life.

Islam not only is not opposed to knowledge; it calls people to strive for knowledge and education. The best example is the epoch in which Arabian science flourished during the Middle Ages, when there was a close union between the Islamic religion and science. Today, the true Muslim culture is capable of helping to establish a society based on knowledge, exactly as it was at the end of the first millennium and in the beginning of the second millennium AD. The Islamic world in the 7th to 11th centuries paved the way for the progress of civilization and it can do this again. But it is necessary to do this using the art of peace, not war.

According to Imam Muslim Hajji, Muslims should raise children according to Islamic canons, but at the same time not isolate them from other educational systems and cultures of the world. Such a system of upbringing and education is an integral part of the Muslim way of life, with such features as originality and its own system of ideological coordinates that are, in many respects, quite dissimilar from the Western system. One has to bring the attention of American experts to the fact that the predominant method of raising the "younger generation" in Arab-Muslim families embraces an authoritative style combined with a high degree of respect for and protection of a child's individuality.

According to Imam Muslim Hajji, one can distinguish two types of educational influences:
1. Primary ones: family and school
2. Secondary ones: mosque, cultural societies, clubs, and so on.

FAMILY UPBRINGING

Islam pays a great deal of attention to the family, as it is the most important educational influence. The family upbringing forms the moral basis of an individual. Secondary educational institutions can strengthen and support this basis, and sometimes correct it, but they never can replace the influence of family upbringing.

The duty of every Muslim is to distinguish truth from lies, light from darkness, and good from evil. The duty of parents is to teach children how to do this. Advice and instructions are useless if they are not based on strong connections between the child and the mentor. Parents should teach children to pray (namaz), to remember Allah (zikr), to address Allah with prayer (dua), to read the Qur'an, and so on. One should not force children to adopt this or that sort of particular religious behavior without explaining to them its essence, its moral, social and cultural purposes. One of the reasons that youths refuse to pray is because they perceive prayer only as a ritual behavior without understanding its true nature. Therefore, one needs to show children the deep sense of prayer and its profound influence on human life. It is desirable that parents talk constantly with children about this subject, until they realize the sense and necessity of each form of worship and experience its beneficial impact on their soul. Eventually, children should come to understand that the main reward is that Allah the Almighty is pleased with them.

A family dialogue implies that questions are asked by all its participants. Questions for discussion should be formulated in an interesting fashion, clearly and precisely, so they do not confuse children. The dialogue between parents and children should help develop the children's intellectual skills. Parents should help their child to formulate questions and encourage him to probe matters. One should not leave the child's complicated questions unanswered, reasoning that he is still young and will not understand anything; one has to try to explain things to him simply but plainly and clearly, with interesting examples. Adults should also train children to search on their own for answers to the questions that life poses, resorting to the help of books and literature.

The proper way to conduct a conversation in a Muslim family includes the following:
- one should not interrupt the person who is speaking. One needs to postpone his question until the speaker finishes his statement; one should not interrupt a child, even if he makes mistakes;
- one should help and encourage a child to express his opinion. This will strengthen his self-confidence; a child needs to see that adults listen to him and sympathize with him;
- it is necessary to train a child to be open and truthful.

Parents should:
- show calmness and magnanimity toward the child;
- listen attentively to what the child says;
- speak the truth, even during a game, because the child will imitate the parent in everything;
- always smile at their child.

According to Imam Muslim Hajji, instructional stories play an important role in a child's upbringing. These stories teach a child about the actions of prophets, heroes and outstanding persons (scholars, preachers, etc.). One should choose age-appropriate stories for a child, which take into account his needs. This is very important for teenagers, when a child especially needs inspiring and vivid examples. Parents should be sensitive to the particular aspects of a child's character and interests, observing what his reaction is to instructional stories or the books he reads. Parents should be interested in a child's opinion on heroes and their actions in various situations. Parents should also ask a child how he would behave in similar situations. One should not dwell on details that are unclear to a child. It is better to begin a story by posing a question to a child, in order to evoke interest in him and to encourage him to listen attentively. One can ask questions during the story with the same purpose. At the end of the story, one should draw instructive conclusions from it.

Parents should develop a child's skills of comparison and analysis, drawing parallels between events in the story and events from the child's life. When criticizing something, parents should explain why it is bad and the danger it poses, so that the child does not aspire to immoral behavior.

UPBRINGING AND EDUCATION IN TOLERANT ISLAM AT SCHOOL; IMAN (FAITH) LESSONS

According to Imam Muslim Hajji, the school should adhere to the regulations of Islam, which states that the search for knowledge is the duty of every Muslim. The programs of religious education at a Muslim school should include following topics:

1. Teaching proper behavior to a pupil
A pupil should first clear his soul of vicious moral and disgraceful qualities. A pupil should get rid of everything that distracts him from learning, diverts his thoughts, and impairs his ability to comprehend reality.

A pupil should obey a teacher just as a patient obeys a doctor.

2. Teaching brotherhood and friendship with different types of people
Using verses from the Qur'an, quotations from Sunnah, and concrete examples from the lives of good people, a teacher should demonstrate to pupils that acceptance is the fruit of good behavior, and bad behavior leads to dissociation. The consequence of good behavior is mutual love, whereas bad behavior results in mutual hatred, envy, and the destruction of relations.

A Muslim should not discuss the shortcomings of his brother or other people. A believer should not think badly of other people, for evil thoughts are a form of abuse, and this is forbidden. In other words, one should not interpret people's actions uncharitably, if there is any possibility to interpret them more generously. If bad things are obvious and beyond doubt, they should be viewed, if possible, as the result of carelessness or forgetfulness. Evil thoughts encourage suspicion and attempts to find out more.

A person's faith is not perfect until he wishes the same things for other people that he wishes for himself, and until he behaves towards others as he wishes that others would behave towards him. If a human heart contains hatred towards a Muslim, it means that the faith of this person is weak; this person is in danger, and his heart is vicious and not ready to meet Allah.

3. About friendship and friendly relations
Not every person can be a friend, but everyone should aspire to possess qualities that would inspire people to be friends with him. What are the qualities that a friend should possess? He should be a sensible man who behaves well. He should not be a troublemaker and should not seek only worldly blessings.

One should give sincere advice to a friend, brother or acquaintance. Explaining things to a person who does not understand them demonstrates compassion, which helps to win over the hearts of wise people. As for fools, one should not pay attention to them.

A person who dwells on the blameworthy acts you have done, or on your blameworthy qualities, is similar to a person who draw your attention to a snake hiding under your clothes, which wishes to kill you.

As for the person who does something openly and deliberately, one should deal with him as cautiously as possible, sometimes giving him advice by means of a hint and sometimes directly, but, in any event, in a way that will not alienate the person.

If your friend, acquaintance, or brother does not pay attention to your advice and continues to behave as before, being unable to overcome his nature, in this case it is best to remain silent.

A censure that is stated confidentially is better than breaking off relations; a hint is better than an open statement; correspondence is better than conversation, and a demonstration of patience is best of all.

4. Forgiveness of mistakes and blunders

Advice should be given gently to one who has committed an oversight in the sphere of religion and inter-religious relations. It is better to forgive and tolerate oversights that alienate people. Muslims say that one needs to find seventy justifications for a mistake by your brother, and if your heart does not accept any of them, reproach yourself.

You should tolerate three things from friends: injustices committed in anger, injustices stemming from excessive informality in a relationship, and injustices done by mistake.

5. Loyalty and sincerity in relations

Loyalty means constancy in love towards comrades, brothers, and friends until death. And following their death, it means maintaining good relations with their children and friends. For one should seek love for the sake of eternal peace. If love ceases before death comes, then the life-work of a person has been wasted, and his aspirations will lead to nothing. Loyalty to a brother in faith means taking care of his friends, dear ones and all those connected with them. One of the results of friendship for the sake of Allah is an absence of envy in religious and material affairs. How can a person envy his brother if everything that his brother owns is also for his benefit?

Loyalty is demonstrated when a person's relationships to the people surrounding him do not change even if he reaches a lofty position and attains great power. On the other hand, if a change of circumstances causes a person to act arrogantly toward his friends, this is a sign of meanness of spirit.

6. Condescendance in relations

Brothers in faith and friends have no right to act condescendingly toward each other. One should not oblige a brother to do something that may be too difficult for him to accomplish. One needs to lighten his burdens and help him. One should not seek to burden others with one's own tasks.

One can acquire natural manners only when a person is humble and considers himself to be less worthy than his brothers, and holds them in high regard. If a person believes that he is better than another, this means that this person despises the other, which is blameworthy.

7. *The necessity to consult with people*
A person demonstrates confidence and inner freedom when he consults with brothers, friends, and other people about actions he plans to take and is open to their advice.

8. *Rules of communication with different people*
When you visit a place, you should enter with a greeting, according to the rules of decency. One should sit in an empty seat. One should show as much humility as possible. It is necessary to be benevolent both toward a friend and an enemy. One should behave with dignity, sit calmly, observing the *adabs* (rules) of communication with different people. At meetings, one should behave calmly, speak in measured tones, and listen to good words without showing excessive delight.

It is best to abstain from jokes. One should not brag. One also should not decorate oneself like a woman. One should not persistently insist on something. If a dispute arises with somebody, it is better to behave with dignity, curb one's arrogance, be patient, consider all sides of an argument, and not gesticulate much. One should begin speaking only when the other person has calmed down. One should not respect a person's wealth more than his honor.

It is necessary to help those who are weak, oppressed, and suffering from misfortune. It is necessary to show the proper way to those who stray from it, to answer greetings, to give to charity, to encourage everything approved by Islam and to keep away from everything forbidden by it.

In no circumstances should one make fun either of a wise man or a foolish man, for a wise person can begin hating, and foolish one can become impudent.

Iman (Faith) lessons for an educational program of tolerant Islam

Part 1
1. My God is Allah
2. Allah is Forgiving and Merciful
3. Allah is the only one and unique
4. We believe in Allah the Almighty
5. Muhammad is the Prophet of Allah
6. The Holy Qur'an
7. We believe in the Qur'an
8. Islam, pillars of Islam
9. Core concepts of Islam
10. Belief in Allah
11. The Doomsday
12. On the value of prayers and worship
13. Muslim holidays, their meanings
14. *Zakat*
15. Islam is the religion of love and brotherhood
16. True Islam
17. Instructions
18. Paradise and Hell
19. Islam is the worship of Allah
20. Bases of belief in Allah
21. The basic qualities of Islam
22. Eternal life

Part 2. Morality of Islam
1. *Adabs* (rules) toward Allah the Almighty
2. *Adabs* toward the Holy Qur'an
3. *Adabs* toward the Prophet (PBUH)
4. *Adabs* toward the Messenger's companions (*ashabs*)
5. *Adabs* for a mosque
6. Personal *adabs*
   A). Self education, moral perfection
   - *Iman* (Faith) in Allah; fulfillment of approved actions;
   - abstention from sinful things;

- purification of intentions; moderateness of desires; abstention from arrogance and pride; carrying out all this by praying to the Almighty;
- remembering Allah as frequently as possible;
- cleanliness, which is divided into two parts: external and internal. External cleanliness means neatness of clothes, cleanliness of other goods and things, moderation. Internal cleanliness implies that a Muslim should believe without any hesitation that no one is equal to Allah, that He is the only one and has no companions. It also means repentance for sins. Every Muslim is obliged to maintain cleanliness of public places and streets.

A). *Adabs* of visiting the toilet;

B). *Adabs* of using *miswak*;[201]

C). *Adabs* of nature (i.e. circumcision of a boy's foreskin, caring for moustaches, wearing a beard, cleanliness of genital regions, shaving off underarm hair, clipping nails; these should be followed in the prescribed manner on certain days of the week, as a rule, on Thursdays);

D). *Adabs* of dreams (how to go to bed)

E). *Adabs* of eating food

F). *Adabs* of dressing

G). *Adabs* of behavior on a trip (travel)

7. *Adabs* of a person in maintaining relations with various people:

A). *Adabs* toward parents

B). *Adabs* with children

C). *Adabs* between spouses

D). *Adabs* with relatives

E). *Adabs* with neighbors

F). *Adabs* with friends

G). *Adabs* with other Muslims

H). *Adabs* of appeal to belief in Allah

I). *Adabs* of the search for knowledge and education

J). *Adabs* of asking for permission

K). *Adabs* of keeping up relations of consent, brotherhood and friendship with different categories of people

L). *Adabs* with disbelievers

M). *Adabs* with animals

8. Moral, praiseworthy qualities
- Sincerity, truthfulness
- *Amanat*[202]
- Restraint, patience
- Good manners
- Generosity
- Salutary qualities
- Justice
9. Blameworthy qualities
- Mendacity
- Misuse; intentional, deliberate crime
- arrogance, vanity
- envy
- hatred
- lying, perjury, false promises, conversations about false things
- disclosure of secrets
- sneers, mockeries, inappropriate jokes
- damnations; pretentiousness of speech
- arguments, disputes and verbal altercations
- superfluous words (verbosity)
- conversations on a topic that does not concern a person.

MUSLIM EDUCATION IN SUPPLEMENTARY INSTITUTIONS

According to Imam Muslim Hajji, Muslim supplementary educational institutions include the mosque, kindergarten, sports and cultural centers, youth and other public organizations.

The mosque should be the family's best assistant and support in fulfilling its educational functions. It should provide parents with a worthy example and give them the feeling of how great and noble is the responsibility that has assigned to them. They will be asked how well they coped with this responsibility on the Judgment Day. The mosque conducts classes and provides sermons that consider the reasons why children disobey, methods to improve this situation, and ways to prevent the decay of the Muslim family. Sermons in a mosque should also examine the reasons why children do not attend mosque and ways to eliminate them.

Parents should pay attention to the translation of the summary of a Friday sermon and weekly lesson, so that children have access to religious instructions. Part of the sermon is in Arabic, and another part in the local language. From time to time, parents should take small children to the mosque.

Many Muslim children living in Western countries suffer from spiritual conflict. In order to help them, one should explain that living in Europe is a necessity and that this does not contradict Islam. In saying this, one should make it clear that the European laws and customs do not permit Muslims to violate the laws of Islam (for example, the prohibition on drinking alcohol and committing adultery). However, there are some exceptional cases (such as regarding the hijab, or head scarf), in which it may be necessary to obey Western customs and laws.

CONCLUSION

The methods that Central Asian Islamic educators have devised for promoting tolerant Islam in their countries should provide valuable food for thought for U.S. policymakers who are concerned about the problems caused by widespread Wahhabi instruction in Muslim schools around the world, which encourages militant radicalism and can lead to terrorism. Central Asian Islamic educators have devised detailed materials appropriate for the primary school, secondary school, and university levels. We can learn much from their experience about how to combat Wahhabism in Islamic educational systems.

SOME POLICY RECOMMENDATIONS

It is my hope that this book presents some unorthodox, but nonetheless valuable, ideas gleaned from Central Asia's anti-Wahhabi academics, politicians and religious leaders. I believe their efforts must be harnessed in an aggressive manner, and their practitioners made active partners in the U.S. fight against radical Islamist ideology.

Specifically, I propose:

- Via USAID and American foundations, to support the publication of textbooks and curriculums composed by Central Asian experts in local languages, to be used in Central Asian schools for lessons on ethics and faith, which incorporate the ideas of tolerant Islam. These textbooks later could be translated into Arabic, English and other Middle Eastern languages to be used in schools and *madrassas* in Afghanistan, Iraq and other Muslim countries.
- To set up talk show programs at local private Central Asian TV and radio stations, and participate in composing and recording audio and video sermons and programs in local languages to be used in Central Asian broadcasting radio and TV network (that may be translated into Arabic, English and other Middle Eastern languages). The sermons and programs should be directed against the ideology of al-Qaeda and other militant Islamists.
- To help assemble a network of moderate Islamic clerics and proponents of the United States in Central Asia, who would be willing to participate in conferences, seminars and mass media events sponsored by U.S. participants in the "battle of ideas."

ENDNOTES

[1] *Saudi Publications on Hate Ideology Invade American Mosques* (Washington, DC: Freedom House, Center for Religious Freedom, 2006), 8.

[2] Alex Alexiev, "Wahhabism: State-Sponsored Extremism Worldwide," Testimony before the United States Senate Committee on the Judiciary, Subcommittee on Terrorism, Technology and Homeland Security, June 26, 2003.

[3] *Changing Minds, Winning Peace: Report of the Advisory Group on Public Diplomacy for the Arab and Muslim World* (Washington, DC: Government Printing Office, October 2003), 15.

[4] Roald Sagdeev and Susan Eisenhower, *Central Asia: Conflict, Resolution, and Change* (Washington, DC: The Eisenhower Institute, 1995), 183.

[5] Notably, it is difficult to find truly democratic regimes, even among   Muslim allies of the United States. A 2005 survey by Freedom House notes that just ten of the world's 47 Muslim-majority countries are true electoral democracies. See David R. Sands, "Finding Allies Within Islam," Washington Times, April 17, 2005.

[6] *History of Bukhara* (Tashkent: 1976), 50.

[7] Ibid.

[8] Ibidem.

[9] Alexandra Bennigsen and Marie Broxup, *The Islamic Threat to the Soviet State* (New York: St. Martin's Press, 1983), 2.

[10] E. Fedorova, "Early Islam, Its Social Meaning and Historic Role," in *Science and Religion* (Moscow) no. 10 (1971), 58.

[11] Bennigsen and Broxup, 17

[12] Ibid.

[13] Ibidem, 2-3.

[14] Michael Rywkin, *Moscow's Muslim Challenge: Soviet Central Asia*, rev. ed. (Armonk, NY: M.E. Sharpe, 1990), 10.

[15] A. A. Seminov, "An Overview of the System of Central Administrative Government of the Early Bukhara Kingdom," in *Material on the History of the Tajik and Uzbek Peoples of Central Asia*, 2nd ed. (Stalinabad: 1955), 21.

[16] N. Aziz, *Awakening of the East* (Moscow: 1966), 165.

[17] T. S. Saidbaev, *Islam and Society* (Moscow: Nauka, 1984), 82.

[18] G. Sabdukov, *Knowledge about the Qur'an* (Kazan: 1906), 66.

[19] Alimarin, "A Few Words on the Modern Literature of the Tartars of Kazan," *Journal of the Ministry of Public Education*, no. 1 (1905), 3.

[20] A. A. Seminov, "The History of Bukhara," in S. Ainn, ed., *Reflections* (Moscow: Nauka, 1960), 991.

[21] A. Sadriddin, *Reminiscence* (Moscow-Leningrad: 1960), 816.

[22] A. Metz, *Muslim Renaissance* (Moscow: 1966), 39.

[23] *Turkmen Register* no. 76 (1909).

[24] A. F. Middendorf, *Sketches of the Fergana Valley* (St. Petersburg: np, 1882), 143.

[25] V. I. Lenin, *Complete Works*, 51, 132 (in Russian).

[26] See, for example: B. V. Vagabov, *Islam and the Family* (Moscow: 1974); Nugman Ashirov, *The Evolution of Islam in the USSR*, 2nd ed. (Moscow: Politizdat, 1973), 39-40.

[27] Ashirov, 39-40.

[28] *Musulmane Sovetskogo Vostoka* (Muslims of the Soviet East), nos. 3-4 (1970), 33.

[29] *Voprosy Nauchnogo Ateizma* (Questions of Scientific Atheism) (Moscow), no. 2 (1966), 79.

[30] Ashirov, 43-44.

[31] Ibid., 47-48, 77.

[32] Ibidem.

[33] Ibidem.

[34] Bennigsen and Broxup, 73.

[35] Ashirov, 12.

[36] Ibid., 50.

[37] James Critchlow, "Corruption, Nationalism, and the Native Elites in Central Asia," *Journal of Communist Studies* no. 4 (1988), 150.

[38] Rywkin, *Moscow's Muslim Challenge: Soviet Central Asia*, 150.

[39] *Nezavisimaya Gazeta*, October 14, 1992.

[40] *Pravda Vostoka*, November 1986.

[41] Mikhail Gorbachev, *Perestroika: New Thinking for Our Country and the World* (New York: Harper and Row, 1987).

[42] Ibid.

[43] Bennigsen and Broxup, 77.

[44] Author's interview, Osh, Kyrgyzstan, August 2004.

[45] Author's interview, Dargin settlement no. 20, Kyrgyzstan, August 2004.

[46] *Islam in Kyrgyzstan: Tendencies of Development: Official Report of the State Commission of the Government of the Kyrgyz Republic on Religious Affairs* (Bishkek, 2004), 35.

[47] Author's interview, Osh, Kyrgyz Republic August, 2004.

[48] Author's interview, Dargin settlement no. 20, Kyrgyzstan, August 2004.

[49] Yuri Kulchik, "Central Asia after the Empire: Ethnic Groups,Communities and Problems," in *Central Asia: Conflict, Resolution, and Change* (Washington, DC: The Eisenhower Institute, 1995), 175.

50 Zeyno Baran, S. Frederick Starr and Svante E. Cornell, *Islamic Radicalism in Central Asia and the Caucasus: Implications for the EU* (Washington and Uppsala: Central Asia-Caucasus Institute and Silk Road Studies Program, 2006), 18.

51 Author's interview, Tashkent, Uzbekistan, July 2004.

52 Author's interview, Tashkent, Uzbekistan, July 2004.

53 Author's interview, Osh, Kyrgyzstan, August 2004.

54 Alexiev, Testimony before the United States Senate Committee on the Judiciary, Subcommittee on Terrorism, Technology and Homeland Security.

55 *Observer* (London), November 24, 2002.

56 Ibid.

57 *Islamic Radicalism in Central Asia and the Caucasus: Implications for the EU,* 20-21.

58 *Literaturnaya Gazeta* (Moscow), June 2, 1990.

59 The *fatwa* is published on the Web site "Islam.ru" by Muhammad-rasul Saaduev, the Chairman of the Expert Council of the Spiritual Department of the Muslims in Dagestan.

60 Muhammad ibn Abd al-Wahhab, *Unforgivable Sins* (Riyadh: The Ministry of Islamic Affairs, Endowments, Proselytization and Guidance of the Kingdom of Saudi Arabia, second edition, 1420AH/1999) (in Arabic).

61 Muhammad ibn Abd al Wahhab, *Kitab at-Tauhid* ("The Book Monotheism")(Riyadh: Ministry of Islamic Affairs, Endowments, Proselytization and Guidance of Kingdom of Saudi Arabia, 1419AH/1998), 17 (in Arabic).

62 Imam ibn Udoma al-Maksidi, *Lumyat al-iytikad* (A Gleam of Belief) (Riyadh: 1419AH/1999), 42 (in Arabic).

63 Muhammad Qutb, *Muqarrir ilm at-Tauhid* (Report on the Knowledge of Monotheism) (Riyadh: The General Presidency for Teaching Girls in the Kingdom of Saudi Arabia, 1412AH/1991), 194 (in Arabic).

64 Ibid., 196.

65 Shaykh ul-islam Taqi al-Din Ahmad ibn Taymiya al-Harrani, *Majmuat al-Fatawa* (Collection of Fatwas) (Riyadh: Kingdom of Saudi Arabia Agency Supervising Publishing Houses, Publications and Distributions, volumes 7-8, 1997), 39 (in Arabic).

66 Abdarrahman Ben'asan ibn Muhammad ibn Abd al-Wahhab. *Opening Knowledge for Comment on Books of Monotheism*, 4th edition (Riyadh CA, 1419AH/1999) (Arabic), 471 (in Arabic).

67 Shaykh Abd al-Aziz ben Abdallah ben Baz, *Bayan at-tauhid* (Statement of Monotheism) (Riyadh: 1417AH/1996), 22 (in Arabic).

68 Muhammad ibn Dzhamil Zinu, *Islamic Aqidah as Stated in the Holy Qur'an and Authentic Sunnah,* (Moscow: Badr Publishing House, 2003), 72 (in Russian).

[69] Imam Muhammad ibn Abd al-Wahhab, *Kashfash-Shubuhaat* (Elimination of Doubts) (Riyadh: The Ministry of Islamic Affairs, Endowments, Proselytization and Guidance of the Kingdom of Saudi Arabia, 1420AH/1999), 13 (in Arabic).

[70] Shaykh ul-islam Taqi al-Din Ahmad ibn Taymiya al-Harrani, *Majmuat al-Fatawa* (Collection of Fatwas) (Riyadh: Kingdom of Saudi Arabia Agency Supervising Publishing Houses, Publications and Distributions, volumes 5-6, 1997), 192 (in Arabic).

[71] Abdul Rahman Ben Hammad Al-Omar, *The Religion of Truth* (Riyadh: The Ministry of Islamic Affairs, Endowments, Proselytization and Guidance of the Kingdom of Saudi Arabia, 1416AH/1995), 23 (in Arabic).

[72] Takijuddin Ahmad Ben Tajmijja al-Kharanij. *Majmuat al-Fatawa* (Collection of Fatwas) (Riyadh: Kingdom of Saudi Arabia Agency Supervising Publishing Houses, Publications and Distributions, volumes 3-4, 1997), 11 (in Arabic).

[73] Abdurrahman Ben Nasyr as-Saadij, *Several Appetizing Fruits from Sermons from a Podium and the Sermon from a Podium at the Proper Place* vol. 3 (Riyadh: 1412AH/1991), 229-230 (in Arabic).

[74] Taqi al-Din Nabhanii, *Nizam al'-Islam* (The System of Islam), fifth edition (np, 1953), 15 (in Arabic).

[75] Abdarrahman Ben'asan Ben Muhammad Ben Abd al-Wahhab, *Fath al-majid li sharh kita bat-tauhid* (Opening Knowledge for Comment on "Books of Monotheism"), fourth edition (Riyadh: CA, 1419AH/1999), 88 (in Arabic).

[76] Muhammad Qutb, *Muqarrir ilm at-Tauhid* (Report on the Knowledge of Monotheism) (Riyadh: The General Presidency for Teaching Girls in the Kingdom of Saudi Arabia, 1412AH/1991), 196 (in Arabic).

[77] Abdullah ben Ibrahim al-Husaym et al., *Monotheism* (Riyadh: The Ministry of Education of the Kingdom of Saudi Arabia, 1411AH/1991), 54 (in Arabic).

[78] Abderrahman Ben Muhammed Ben Kasym al'-Hanbalii an-Nadzhdii, *Shaykh ul-Islam Muhammad ibn Abd al-Wahhab; Hashiya al'-usul as-salasa* (Shaykh ul-Islam Muhammad ibn Abd al-Wahhab: Notes on Three Main Principles) (Riyadh: 1418AH/1997), 27, 29 (in Arabic).

[79] Dr. Yusus Ardaui, *Al-halal va al-haram fi al-Islam* (Permitted and Forbidden Things in Islam) (np: Dar ash-Shahab, 1986), 160 (in Arabic).

[80] an-Nadzhdii, 27.

[81] al-Wahhab, *Kitab at-Tauhid*, 45.

[82] Abd al-Aziz bin Abdallah bin Baz, *Vujub al-amal bisunnatir-rasul va kufru mann ankaraha* (The Necessity of Obeying the Sunnah of Allah's Messenger and Declaring Those who Deny it to be Apostates) (Riyadh: The Ministry of Islamic

Affairs, Endowments, Proselytization and Guidance of the Kingdom of Saudi Arabia, 1420AH/1999), 27 (in Arabic).

[83] Muhammad ibn Salih al'-'Useimin, *The Faith of the Adherents of the Sunnah and the United Muslim Community*, nd, 15 (in Russian).

[84] Abid Tawfiq al-Hashimi, *Aqidah al-yahud fi Falastin wa Tanfiduha Qur'anan wa Injilan wa Ta'rikhan* (The Jewish Doctrine to Occupy Palestine: Critique from the Perspective of the Qur'an, Torah, Bible and History) (np: Library of "Umm al-Qura," 1990), 26 (in Arabic).

[85] Muti' an-Nuvnav, *Al-Islam val-hayat. Ta'rih va hadara* (Islam and Life: History and Culture) (Riyadh, 1417AH), 33 (in Arabic).

[86] al-Hashimi, *Aqidah al-yahud fi Falastin wa Tanfiduha Qur'anan wa Injilan wa Ta'rikhan*, 125.

[87] Qutb, *Muqarrir ilm at-Tauhid*, 140.

[88] Zinu, *Islamic Aqidah as Stated in the Holy Qur'an and Authentic Sunnah*, 67.

[89] al-Hashimi, 67.

[90] Muti' an-Nuvnav, *Al-Islam val-hayat. Ta'rih va hadara.* (Islam and Life: History and Culture) (Riyadh, 1417AH), 90 (in Arabic).

[91] Muhammad ibn Dzhamil Zinu, *Islamic Aqidah as Stated in the Holy Qur'an and Authentic Sunnah*, (Moscow: Badr Publishing House, 2003) (Russian) 31.

[92] Ibid. 32.

[93] Ibidem, 77.

[94] Abdul Rahman ben Hammad Al-Omar, *The Religion of Truth* (Riyadh: The Ministry of Islamic Affairs, Endowments, Proselytization and Guidance of the Kingdom of Saudi Arabia, 1416AH/1995) (Arabic) p111-113.

[95] Author's interview, July 2005.

[96] Abdul Rahman ben Hammad al-Omar, *Din al-Haq* (The Religion of Truth) (Riyadh: The Ministry of Islamic Affairs, Endowments, Proselytization and Guidance of the Kingdom of Saudi Arabia, 1420 AH), 56 (in Russian).

[97] Ibid., 116

[98] Imam Muhammad ibn Abd al-Wahhab, *Kashfash-Shubuhaat* (The Elimination of Doubts) (Riyadh: The Ministry of Islamic Affairs, Endowments, Proselytization and Guidance of the Kingdom of Saudi Arabia, 1420AH/1999), 37 (in Arabic).

[99] Qutb, *Muqarrir ilm at-Tauhid*, 240.

[100] Sayid Abul A'l a Mawdudi, *Let Us Be Muslims* (Jeddah: IQRA charitable organization, 1997), 52-53 (in Russian).

[101] Ibid., 62.

[102] Ibidem, 69.

[103] Ibidem, 179.

[104] Salih ibn Fawzan al-Fawzan, *The Book of Monotheism* (Makhachkala: Badr, 2003), 58 (in Russian).

[105] Ibid., 60

[106] Qutb, *Muqarrir ilm at-Tauhid*, 60.

[107] Muti' an-Nuvnav, *Al-Islam val-hayat. Ta'rih va hadara* (Islam and Life: History and Culture) (Riyadh, 1417AH, nd), 68 (in Arabic).

[108] Taqi al-Din Nabhanii, *Nizam al'-Islam* (The System of Islam), fifth edition (np, 1953), 28 (in Arabic).

[109] Ibid., 40.

[110] Ibid., 64.

[111] Muhammad Qutb, *Svetskiye Lyudi i Islam* (Civic People and Islam) (Badr, nd), 5 (in Russian).

[112] Ibid., 219

[113] Mawdudi, *Let us be Muslims*, 86-87.

[114] Nabhanii *Nizam al'-Islam*, 64-66.

[115] Ibid., 67-68.

[116] Qutb, *Svetskiye Lyudi i Islam*, 115.

[117] Nabhanii, *Nizam al'-Islam*, 144.

[118] Qutb, *Svetskiye Lyudi i Islam*, 72.

[119] Ibid., 82.

[120] Ibidem, 84.

[121] Ibidem, 94.

[122] Mohammed ibn Abd-ur-Rahman Humeis, *Shirk i Ego Prichini*, (Badr, 1999) http://www.islam-ru.com/04UBEJDENIE/STATYI/tavkhid_st_003.htm.

[123] Qutb, *Muqarrir ilm at-Tauhid*, 232.

[124] Wahbiy Suleyman Gaudji al-Albani, *Al-mar'atu al-muslima* (The Muslim Woman), fourth edition (Riyadh: The General Presidency for Teaching Girls in the Kingdom of Saudi Arabia, fourth edition, 1412AH/1991), 156 (in Arabic).

[125] Maysar bint Yasin, *Makanaki tusyidiy (Make your Dignity Happy)* (United Arab Emirates: np, 2001), 56 (in Arabic).

[126] Ibid., 53.

[127] Yusus Ardaui, *Al-halal va al-haram fi al-Islam* (Permitted and Forbidden Things in Islam) (Dar ash-Shahab, 1986), 151 (in Arabic).

[128] Ibid., 152.

[129] Audiotape distributed among Central Asian pilgrims who visited Saudi Arabia for the Hajj in 2004

[130] Yasin, *Makanaki tusyidiy*, 21.

[131] Ibid., 23-25.

[132] Yusus Ardaui, *Fatawa muasyra* (Fatwas of the Modern World), seventh edition (Dar al-vafaa lit-tibaya van-nashr vat-tavzi, 1998), 425 (in Arabic).

[133] Ibid., 267.

[134] Ardaui, *Al-halal va al-haram fi al-Islam* , 10-11.

[135] Yasin, *Makanaki tusyidiy*, 19-21.

[136] Solih ben 'Avzan ben Abdallah al-'Avzan, *The Orientation of Attention to Precepts that Concern Believing Women* {Riyadh: Ministry on Islamic Affairs, Endowments, Proselytization and Guidance of the Kingdom of Saudi Arabia, 1418AH/1998), 14 (in Arabic).

[137] Sayyid Qutb, *War, Peace and Islamic Jihad* (Karachi: International Islamic Publishers Ltd., 1988), 107-142.

[138] Zinu, *Islamic Aqidah According to the Holy Qur'an and Authentic Sunnah*, 99.

[139] *Programs on Studies in Shari'ah Sciences* (Moscow: Joint edition of the Ministry on Islamic Affairs, Endowments, Proselytization and Guidance of the Kingdom of Saudi Arabia and Ibrahim bin Abd al-Aziz Al Ibrahim Foundation, 1999), 21.

[140] Muti' an-Nuvnav, *Al-Islam val-hayat. Ta'rih va hadara* (Islam and Life: History and Culture) (Riyadh, 1417AH), 85 (in Arabic).

[141] Qutb, *Muqarrir ilm at-Tauhid*, 78.

[142] Hanafi Abdullah al-Hanafi and Muhammad Muharram al-Misri, *The Literature Texts*, eighth edition (Riyadh: The Ministry of Education of the Kingdom of Saudi Arabia, 1408AH/1988), 110 (in Arabic).

[143] al-Hanafi and al-Misri, *The Literature Texts*, 54.

[144] an-Nadzhdii, *Shaykh ul-Islam Muhammad ibn Abd al-Wahhab: Hashiya al'-usul as-salasa*, 118.

[145] Abdurrahman Ben Nasyr as-Saadij, *Al'-favakih ash-shahiiya val-hutab al'-minbariiya val-hitab al'-minbariiya 'ala al'-munasabat* (Several Appetizing Fruits from Sermons from a Podium and the Sermon from a Podium in the Proper Place) (Riyadh, 1412AH/1991), 244 (in Arabic).

[146] an-Nadzhdii, *Shaykh ul-Islam Muhammad ibn Abd al-Wahhab: Hashiya al'-usul as-salasa*,135.

[147] Ibid.. 136

[148] al-Wahhab, *Unforgivable Sins*, 14.

[149] al-Omar, *Din al-Haqq*, 99.

[150] Ardaui, *Fatawa muasyra*, 289.

[151] Mawdudi, *Let us be Muslims*, 286-287.

[152] Ibid., 153.

[153] Zinu, *Islamic Aqidah as Stated in the Holy Qur'an and Authentic Sunnah*, 29.

[154] Abdarrahman Ben'asan ben Muhammad ben Abd al-Wahhab, *Fath al-majid li sharh kita bat-tauhid* (Opening Knowledge for Comment on the "Books of Monotheism"), fourth edition (Riyadh: CA, 1419AH/1999), 136 (in Arabic).

[155] Zinu, *Islamic Aqidah as Stated in the Holy Qur'an and Authentic Sunnah*, 131-133.

[156] as-Saadij, *Several Appetizing Fruits from Sermons from a Podium and the Sermon from a Podium in the Proper Place*, 241-244.

[157] Ardaui, *Fatawa muasyra*, 286.

[158] Sulayman ben Abdulaziz ad-Duwaysh, *Wasa'il at-Targ'iyb wa anwa'uhu fiy Da'vati an-Nabiy* (Methods of Agitation in the Proselytization of the Prophet Muhammad) (Riyadh: 1418AH/1997), 28 (in Arabic).

[159] Zinu, *Islamic Aqidah according to the Holy Qur'an and Authentic Sunnah*, 76-77.

[160] Ibid.; M. A. Ibrahim, Establishing the Laws of Allah (Makhachkala: Badr, 1997); Abd al-Aziz bin Baz, The Necessity of Obeying the Sunnah of Allah's Messenger and Declaring Those who Deny it to be Apostates, (Riyadh: General Department of Printing of the Waqf Ministry, 2000).

[161] Abd al-Aziz bin Baz, *The Necessity of Obeying the Sunnah of Allah's Messenger and Declaring Those who Deny it to be Apostates* (Riyadh: General Department of Printing of the *Waqf* Ministry, 2000), 35.

[162] Author's interview, Cholpon-Ata, Kyrgyzstan, August 2004.

[163] Imam al-Bukhari, *Sahih Bukhari* (Ummah Publishing House, 2003), hadith 56.

[164] Vladimir Soloviev, *Muhammad: His Life and Religious Teaching* (St. Petersburg, np, 1902), 78.

[165] G. Miloslavsky, "People of Other Religions of the Book," in E. Kozhokina and V. Maksimenko, eds., *Islam and Islamism* (Moscow: RISI, 1999), 26.

[166] Author's interview, Cholpon-Ata, Kyrgyzstan, August 2004.

[167] Ibid.

[168] *Forty Hadiths of An-Nawawi* (Riyadh: International Islamic Publishing House, 1992), 38.

[169] Ibid., Chapter 266, hadith 1559.

[170] Ibidem, Chapter 274, hadith 1577.

[171] Ibidem, Chapter 27. 54.

[172] *Shari'ah* (Bishkek: np, 1994), 119.

[173] *Al-Aschab* (or *as-sahaba*)—followers, companions of the Prophet; people, who communicated closely with him or took part in his campaigns. Later, *sahaba* were called those people who saw the Prophet Muhammad once, even in his childhood.

[174] Author's interview, September 2004.

[175] Ibid.

[176] N.O. Osmanov,*The Qur'an, Translation from Arabic with comments* (Qom: Sayyid Mojtaba Musavi Lari Foundation of Islamic C.W., 1992).

[177] "Tafsir" is the interpretation of Qur'anic texts by Islamic experts.

[178] An-Nawawi, *The Gardens of the Righteous* (Moscow: Badr, 2001), Chapter 3, hadith 194, 121.

[179] Ibid., hadith 265.

[180] Favzan, *The Book of Monotheism*, 49.

[181] *Forty Hadiths of An-Nawawi*, 53.

[182] Author's interview, August 2004.

[183] al-Bukhari, *Sahih Bukhari*, 486.

[184] An-Nawawi, *The Gardens of the Righteous*, 34.

[185] al-Bukhari, *Sahih Bukhari*, hadith 1932.

[186] Reinhardt Dozy, "Islamic Dogma and Divine Worship" in A.E. Krymskiy, *History of Muhammadanism*, (Moscow: np, 2003, reprint of 1904 edition), 270-271.

[187] *The Meaning and Sense of the Qur'an* vol. 5 (Munich: SKD Bavaria Verlag & Handel GmbH), 2648.

[188] The *fatwa* is published on the website www.islam.ru by Muhammad-Rasul Saaduev, the Chairman of the Experts' Council of the Religious Administration of Muslims of Dagestan.

[189] Sayyid Afandi Chirkeysky, *Who are the Wahhabis?* (Makhachkala: Mazhmatul Favvid, 1997), 3.

[190] Author's interview, August 2004.

[191] *Changing Minds, Winning Peace*, 15.

[192] Some years ago, this subject was the topic of the author's PhD dissertation. See "Problem of Studies of the Village Elite in the Social Science of Developing Countries, (Case study of Egypt)," in *Developing Countries: Studies of Social Problems (The Theory of Social Structure)* (Moscow: USSR Academy of Sciences, Institute of Oriental Studies, NAUKA Publishing House, 1978), 117-135.

[193] Imam Muslim, "Recommendations for American Radio and Television Journalists," American Foreign Policy Council Central Asia Counterterrorism Project, http://www.afpc.org/cac/recommendations.pdf.

[194] Ibid.

[195] Ibidem.

[196] Ibidem.

[197] al-Bukhari, *Sahih Bukhari*, Chapter 12.

[198] American Foreign Policy Council Central Asia Counterterrorism Project, http://www.afpc.org/cac/cac_publications.shtml.

[199] Author's interview, Tashkent, Uzbekistan, July 2004.

[200] American Foreign Policy Council Central Asia Counterterrorism Project, http://www.afpc.org/cac/cac_publications.shtml.

[201] *Miswak* is a bush with disinfectant and deodorizing properties.

184

202 The word "amanat" (Arabic) originates from the verb "amana," which means "to believe (in God), in somebody; to trust, entrust." *Amanat* means reliability, fidelity, honesty. In this case, the matter concerns the duty to keep something given in deposit (or as security) in safety and the duty to return it.